Let this page serve as a caution. Children should read this book with parent supervision, if at all.

I regret that there is material for such a book. The abandoned children, the hungry, the abused and neglected. We can discribe an event and stop at the edge before it becomes offensive to our ears and hearts. The children who are abused cannot do so, they must endure the hurt and suffer the pain during and after the event.

So in that vein, I have tried to tell the story of a few and one in particular who lived in that dark world of neglect and hurt.

I did stop on the edge in writing the story on paper. In my mind and heart, the scenes rushed through. I wanted to tell the story but it could not end soon enough, as if by ending my story their story would stop and the pain would go away. I know it never will.

My intention is not to offend anyone. Those who have suffered abuse or traumatic experiences in their life, or those who are prone to depression should not read this book.

The story is a fictional one and rightfully so, a real person should not have to relive any of these experiences. I have tried to insert a little happiness and some level of success in their later years. Some of the bad guys are caught, which is often not the case in real life.

I have done my best to do the project in the right way.

Mother's Coat

Mother's Coat

Milton J Southerland

Self published by Milton J Southerland
2441 Old Hwy 411 South, Chatsworth Georgia 30705

Published in the United States of America

Acknowledgement: Many thanks to my wife Louise for using the little free time she has for reading the manuscript and for her help in editing. Any errors that remain are my own.

ISBN 978-0-578-02289-5

Introduction

The phrase 'children are our most valuable resource' has always struck a bad chord with me.   I never really understood why for years. Maybe, it is because it seems we are putting children on a spreadsheet like fuel and coal reserves or real estate. Children live in the here and now and experience pain and problems just like the rest of humanity. When the future comes, they will surely be the parents, business leaders and protectors of freedom, however, we can not ignore the fact that they are living, breathing individuals who have every right to life as a child (born or unborn) as they will when they are grown.

Ragamuffin is a term made famous in the movies. It refers to a ragged, dirty person. The term was perhaps meant as a pronouncement of the social distance between the well to do and the homeless street child. The pronouncement is, however, not against the child but against a society that allows conditions to exist where a child is forced to live as a ragamuffin.

Today, sixty-million children are abandoned. The figure is a rough estimate and the number is probably much higher. No nation is exempt from embarrassment. Those who may claim to have no children on the street cannot escape the responsibility of the global community where every hungry and homeless child is every adults failure and opportunity to lend a helping hand.

One estimate is that India alone has eighteen million street children while Brazil has twenty million. Eastern Europe is at one million but reports are guesses at best. America is reported to have seven thousand but I wonder about that number. China has one to three million orphans. I hope that means a hot meal for them which is more than street children can expect.

5

My story does not cover the millions. It goes into the lives of only a few. They are not real but the experiences could very well be true for someone. We see the numbers in millions and it is difficult to think about. What can one do for a million? Perhaps we can relate to one or two if I can wrap a story around them.

The story is not just about a few street kids. There were adults involved or at least one in the conception of the child. There was government that encouraged parents to have large families then changed their mind about it or the government changed. I will mention the roving death squads, who go out to clean up the streets by killing the children, but this story is not even about them.

If in these pages, I can bring one small life before us and hold it up for all of us to see. Then, perhaps, we will understand that it is not just millions in the masses but that it is an individual out there on the street begging for a bite to eat. It is an individual child who crawls under a house to be near the warm steam pipes that heat the home.

I almost did not write this story when I thought of the research I would do, the knowledge I would gain, the responsibility I would have to acknowledge once I could no longer say 'I didn't know.'.

There is another side of the coin. For there to be slave trade, there must be buyers of the children. For there to be sex trade, there must be predators to pay the pimp. For there to be exploitation, there must be a permissive government and a society that turns a deaf ear and a blind eye.

If we judge strictly by how well we take care of others, society at large is the real ragamuffin.

Chapter 1

A picture of family perfection made the real estate agent's job easy. They scheduled the visits of prospective buyers so that the over-priced house would take on the aura of a happy home. It never failed to bring out the best in clients.

The agent and her clients, today a young couple, the wife being very pregnant, smiled and received smiles as the happy family living there went about their morning routine. The husband and soon to be father could well afford the house. He was lucky enough to land a job with a new senator. Well, not really luck. He had slaved for over a year getting the senator elected. He had dealt with rumors about the senator, some true, some not putting just the right spin on the stories with the media. Now, it was payday.

Daria was loading laundry into the dryer when they visited the laundry room which was off the kitchen and one floor down. She wore a business suit which showed off her features as she bent to toss in another item of clothing. She took off upstairs to continue her morning routine. The young husband got a punch in the ribs as his eyes lingered too long on the stairs. Then, they also went up the stairs, she breathing hard by the time they reached the top. A grand piano could be seen to their left in the foyer.

The pregnant lady wandered into the kitchen where Daria was making a list of some sort. Perhaps reminders for herself or the family. Her husband admired the piano and struck a few keys which echoed off the acoustics of the wide open area.

Rested now, the couple were herded up another flight of stairs to the bedroom areas. The master bedroom was

7

pristine with the dust free furniture and oversize bed. A plush comforter invited them to touch it as they walked around the room. The full bath with its deep tub and spa jets attracted their attention while the agent patted her foot. She knew every inch of the house and all this glamour was old news to her. She had her face back on by the time the couple came out of the bathroom a little flushed.

Next was what should have been a real estate agents worst nightmare, the teenage daughters room. It was neatly cluttered, just as they had planned. A few stylish articles of clothing were strewn around, the bathroom was littered with makeup and bubble bath bottles. It was done in pink.

Deanna, a gymnast of fourteen years, stood in her bare feet wearing tight jeans and a low-cut pullover. A vest with one button high on her midsection finished off the look of the day. Her mother darted in about that time.

"You can't wear that to school. It shows too much."

The agent and the pregnant lady smiled knowingly while the husband inched toward the door. He was almost pushed aside by Deanna who was sprinting toward the stairs, her mother in pursuit. The discussion was still going on when the couple returned to the ground floor.

"Do as your mother says. You should not run to me every time you disagree with her wishes." A male voice was heard saying. What was not heard were the words spoken in Deanna's ear after her mother went off with other morning chores on her mind.

"Just put something on over until you are dropped off at school. You can adjust your attire in the bathroom as soon as you get there."

Deanna was smiling as she passed the couple on her way back to her room. It seemed to them an unlikely end to a hot discussion. 'Oh, well, teenagers.' They thought. They had a few years before they faced that problem.

Matte Slithers sat at a table in an alcove drinking coffee and reading the morning paper. He was suppose to be there as part of the overall plan. He stood politely to shake hands with the young husband and introduced himself. The young man told him his name and who he worked for. Matte took a mental note of the name and decided to stay in touch. Having the inside track with a senator could be useful someday. He smiled and picked up his paper and coffee cup at the same time. He was not selling the house so he said nothing more. He would look the part of a normal husband and father for a few more minutes. In fact, the role was easy for him. Unknown to anyone else who knew him, he was playing a part. His dedication to his family was surface level only. Although, he did feel like he loved his family. It was good to have a place to come back to and after all, his wife was beautiful and his daughter was very popular in school.

Selling the house was a simple financial maneuver. They would stay close to the neighborhood. The equity that had built up in the house would give them all some fun money and let them step up a notch to a house with a large pool and a private gym and guest house.

They all breathed a sigh of relief after the agent and her clients had left. In fifteen minutes they would all scatter. Deanna was off to school to be dropped off by Daria on her way to work at the foundation.

"How long will you be gone this time?" Daria asked her husband while she checked her appearance in a full length mirror which was mounted on the pantry door.

"Two days, just one night." Matte said looking over the paper.

"I hate these overnight trips." She said.

"So do I but it is part of the job. I can loose at golf more ways than most. That is why I get so many signatures on the dotted line." Matte said.

"I know. You are the best. I'll see you when you get back."

She kissed him on the lips. He pinched her bringing out a little ouch from her lips. He laughed and patted the pinch well again. Daria laughed and headed toward the garage.

"Let's go De." She yelled in the direction of the stairs.

Deanna took the steps three at a time and was on her mother's heels before she got out the door. Her mother smiled at her looking her up and down. She was properly covered. Deanna smiled at her father and he winked from behind his paper.

"Be good, you two." He said.

"You got it." Deanna said.

"You too." Daria yelled.

Matte watched the car pull out of the driveway as he took out his personal cell phone. One he would replace after the next two days.

"Hello Trunk. Matte here. Is everything set?"

"Yeah man. Be on time. Don't forget the money."

"I'm sending you a head shot of me so you will know who I am."

"Remember to can your phone. I don't want any trail leading back to me." Trunk said.

"Got it covered. See you in a few hours." Matte said.

Chapter 2

Trunk was impeccably dressed at all times. Whether it was in a business suit or casual wear, at work or play, he looked good. He was well known and often received a polite nod. The rest, who did not nod, gave him room when he was near them. He was not a public drinker except on a social level at high class establishments. Then, he held himself in check being in control at all times. His home had a well stocked bar and wine cellar. His car was immaculate, a shiny black. Trunk had taken it in trade. A stocky fellow who served as his driver and watchful eye, also looked after the car. He was paid well and talked little. He always stayed with the car for Trunk did not need a body guard, although, he was only a cell phone away if his boss needed him.

They were both products of the street. Situations at home had driven them away and so, as children, they had roamed the streets in search of food. Trunk was the one with the brains to manage so the other accepted his lot, as the underling, without jealousy. Trunk had always saved a portion of his earnings from the street. He never wasted any thing on pleasure. He ate what he needed to survive and bought what he could not scrounge, to look good.

The back seats let down from the inside of the car so Trunk could order a naughty girl into the trunk of the car if she needed discipline. Then, get her out the same way, if a cop got nosey. That is how he got his nickname Trunk. No one knew him by any other name.

He was a good looking man. The driver was too but he was not in the same category with his boss. Trunk had always worked out. At first, he used what ever he could find in the alleys to lift. He would work out every night before dropping off to sleep. In the morning, it was pushups to get him wide awake. The result was an unusually strong man of six feet tall. Other pimps did not mess with him at close range. One had shot him once but Trunk took the gun from him and beat him to death. The cops called it self defense and rightfully so.

If Trunk had a redeeming quality, it was that he operated in an insidious way. He did not push and shove his way into a large business enterprise. He approached business in a seductive way. He enticed those he needed, mostly young women, into serving his wishes doing so in very subtle ways.

His first girl was fresh off the bus from rural America. He watched her for days as she spent the money she had saved. She went door to door looking, first, for modeling and acting jobs. Television and movie theaters were his sales force and he was proud that his advertising budget was zero. Once he saw the girl leave her apartment with her suitcase, he knew it would not be long before she was hungry. He knew most would save a few dollars so they could eat and do their laundry. He washed some clothes at the coin laundry, not because he could not afford a cleaner, but so he could get in close proximity to the girl. She would get use to seeing him and so not be afraid.

Taffy was a pretty thing and only fourteen but she lied her way to seventeen. She had the maturity to pull it off. With her quick smile and giggly energy, she must have been very popular in school.

She grew up in a strict environment. Strict by her standard anyway. She liked to dress like the movie stars with skin tight or loose revealing garments. Her very loving parents did not approve. Neither would they let her stay out for late night parties. All her friends did and they came to school with tales

12

of intimate late night rendezvous. She got details that made her blush but she listened nevertheless to their luscious stories.

After her ninth year in school, Taffy was very bright, she climbed out a window and walked to the bus station, bought a ticket for the city and disappeared from her parents life.

Trunk was only a year older than Taffy but very street wise. He knew teen-talk but also the wise adult talk of one much older. In his environment, he was going to be a player and he knew it. Taffy was his first step to independence.

On that night, he used his teen-talk routine.

"Here you dropped these." Trunk handed her a pair of her underwear.

"I am so embarrassed." Taffy said.

"Ah, don't worry about it. It's no biggee." She blushed anyway.

"If you're gonna' make it in the city, you got t' loosen up a little." He told her.

"I know. It's just that, you know, things are hard."

"Been there." He pulled his clothes from the dryer and started to fold.

Taffy moved a little ways down the table and finished her work. She was about finished but lingered, folding and refolding. After all, she had no place to be. The coin laundry offered some degree of security. It had lights anyway.

"So, how you making out." Trunk raised his voice over the machines still turning. A woman in the corner paid no attention to them.

"Got kicked out of my apartment." Taffy said with her head angled toward her clothes.

"Look. Uh..."

"Taffy." She introduced herself.

"They call me Trunk." He said.

"That's a funny name." She mumbled.

"Ain't it though." He laughed, not taking offense.

"Look Taffy. I don't want to be forward, or anything, but I

have been on the street myself. I can put you up for a few days if you like. No pressure or anything. I just know how it is. What say?" He waited for her answer.

Her stomach growled. She hoped he did not hear it. She was using her last change to clean her clothes. She had to look good for her job search tomorrow.

"Well, just for a few days. I've got some jobs to check on and I know I'll find something soon."

"Of course you will." He encouraged. "Everybody gets down on their luck once in a while."

That was how it started with her and Trunk. The jobs did not pan out. She did not have to go back on the street because Trunk let her stay at his place. He would let her do his books for him. She was good with math. There would not be much pay now but as his business grew, so would her pay. It seemed like a nice arrangement.

Her real age became their secret. Six months after their platonic arrangement began, Trunk and she had a dinner to celebrate her real birthday. She turned fifteen. He took her to a movie and for the first time, they had wine together after they got home. She owed him so much. He had been so kind to her. Because of him, she did not have to sleep on the street. Going home was not an option. So after the dinner and movie and the wine, how could she resist when he led her to his bed. She gave up her purity to a man, no a boy really, and did not know his last name and never would.

Trunk's first step was complete. He had his 'bottom girl'. Taffy would be trained to look after his books and collect from the other girls he would bring into his 'stable'. To her she was his girl now. To him she was the first piece of a puzzle he was putting together. He never told her his big plans and when she asked how he made his money, he told her it was man's business and for her not to worry. All she had to do was keep up with the numbers for him. Later she would be dealing with business partners and customers, but right now she needed to learn the business from the ground up. So, she did. Sometimes she stayed in the apartment and brushed up on accounting. Other times she was on his arm in the pretty clothes he bought her. She was Trunk's girl.

He liked to take pictures of her. He started taking some with her in a new outfit he had bought. He'd snap a picture before they went out for the evening. Then it escalated. He wanted other pictures for himself, so he could keep her near him when he was at work. It was difficult for her at first. The revealing clothes were one thing. Nudity went against all the teaching she had received back home but she soon broke that barrier down since it was just for Trunk. After all, they were in love now.

She got really angry when they were dining with what Trunk called a client and he showed a nude picture of her to the man. Trunk apologized and quickly put it back in his pocket. They had wine and then more wine. Taffy got over being upset and joined in as they drained the bottle then another. Trunk seemed to be having as much fun as anyone but unknown to her or the 'client' he was perfectly sober.

"You are too drunk to drive." Trunk told the client. "You best sleep on our sofa tonight. It pulls out into a bed."

"What ever you say." The man slurred.

Taffy frowned but she had drank so much wine she could not make herself seem serious. Trunk purchased a bottle to go and directed his retinue to his shiny black car where his sober driver was waiting.

They got home safe and sound where Trunk told his driver to take the car and go have some fun. He gave him a wad of cash.

Taffy excused herself leaving the two men alone. The client handed Trunk several hundred dollars. Then Trunk joined Taffy in their bedroom. She was dressed for the occasion by now. Trunk poured her a glass of wine which they drank together while sitting on the side of the bed.

"My friend on the sofa is a very important client to me." He said into her ear. "I want you to go out and make him feel

15

at home."

"I want to stay here." She said.

"It's no big deal. We are still best friends." He said.

"But I love you." She protested.

"I love you too but this is business. Do this one thing for me and we will go shopping tomorrow."

They never went shopping together the next day. He gave her a hundred to do with as she pleased. It was the most money she had owned since leaving her parent's home. When she got home that evening after spending half of the hundred, a young shy little girl was sitting with Trunk at the kitchen table shoveling down scrambled eggs and toast.

"Taffy, this is Sunny," He introduced them, "she is down on her luck and needs a place to stay for a few days. Look after her for me. Will you?"

Taffy turned her head sideways and gave Trunk her most irritated look.

"It is just for a few days, until she can check on a job."

"I understand. Come on Sunny. Let's get you cleaned up."

Taffy did indeed understand and never questioned her instructions again. Each task brought her a portion of the proceeds. She still shared Trunk's bed exclusively, that is until Sunny was fully indoctrinated. Then, she was one of two.

Trunk's cover business was real estate. He helped out of town people find a place to live for a small fee. On one of the occasions when he sent Taffy out to show a place, she found Sunny and Trunk in bed together. He just smiled and told her it was 'no big deal'. He stretched out his hand and she joined them reluctantly. In time, she graduated to the sofa, as all the girls did.

Chapter 3

The rain came down in a torrent. Street gutters ran like fast moving streams as they received water from the slanted roadways. Cars splashed pedestrians unmercifully as they made their way to their destinations or stood waiting for a taxi cab to take them home or to dinner in a fancy restaurant. The streets were darkened as the rain cut off the glare of street lights, mounted on post along the sidewalk.

It was even darker in the alleys and in doorways and parking garages. At the bottom of a stack of concrete steps it was dark and wet. Raised concrete ledges that were meant to make the water flow around the stairs were overwhelmed and so a stream of water ran down the steps toward a drain at the bottom. The drain was only partially open so water would puddle in the four by four square between the retaining wall and the metal door that was locked for the night.

A little hand pulled candy wrappers from the drain in the hope that the water would go down better and not completely flood the small space. The other hand held a pair of ragged shoes to keep them from getting soak through. The treasures were already damp from the rain. Dark hair, made coal black because it was drenched, hung like coarse strings across the small face and over the slender shoulders. The face was pressed into the small corner made by the door facing. An uncontrolled tremble shook the small body. The one garment had already soaked up all the moisture it would hold and became the color of human skin. It was a cold rain that hurt when it hit tender skin.

One eye, big and frightened, peeped through the wet strands of hair, as a shadow, a new shadow, entered the space.

Madra was swept up like a ball player would scoop up a loose ball. A strong hand tucked her under a heavy coat. It was dry there. She shivered from her wet clothes and fear as she was carried around a corner and placed in the trunk of a waiting car. It was warm there too.

Trunk knew Madra well, although they had never met. She had appeared on the street like so many others. She looked to be perhaps eleven years old. For a moment, but not for long, Trunk wondered what tragedy or fiend cast a small person such as this out into a cruel world to look out for themselves. Perhaps, the parents died. Perhaps an orphanage ran out of money or the child had escaped. He did not think along this lines for long. He could not afford to dwell in his line of work. He would test her and in time he might add her to his stable.

He drove the car himself tonight. These affairs were his secret way of making operating capitol for his future endeavors. Only he, Taffy and his clients knew of this part of his work. Well, of course the child knew every detail of the sorted business.

He had heard not a sound from the trunk of his car. She is probably asleep, he thought. For a brief moment he almost pulled over to see if she was still breathing but it was much to wet outside.

Taffy hated these nights. She knew what would come through the door any time now. Her job was to doll up the little girl, put her in a room and calm her fears as best she could, then leave her alone. The next morning she would again clean her up and send her on her way. She always gave the girls a small portion of her earnings for the nights work. It was the least she could do. Except the occasional shutter she felt deep in her soul, she looked on all these events as work now. To do anything else would have meant her sanity.

The building they used for the young girl tricks was off the beaten track. She had cleaned several rooms and painted them herself.   There were curtains and everything. She thought it looked real nice.

Trunk knocked at the door.

"Yes." Taffy said.

"It's me." Trunk said. "It is raining cats and dogs out there."

From under his coat he took out the small bundle that had curled around his huge arm. He sat her on her feet.

"She got me wet to my skin. I'll have to change before I go to the airport." He complained. He went into another room and put on a dry outfit.

'I'll keep the client busy for a couple of hours to give you some extra time. It will take some work to get her ready. You should feed her something. I wouldn't want her to faint from hunger right in the middle of everything. I might have to give a partial refund." He instructed.

"Like you'd do that." Taffy said taking the girl by the hand.

"For repeat clients, you bet." He slammed the door on that last remark leaving no time to argue.

Taffy pulled the girl down the short hallway to a bathroom.

"What's you name?" Taffy asked.

The girl did not reply. She stood there in her wet clothes, looking up with big round eyes and shivering but did not speak.

"Look here. I've got a job to do. Don't make me be stern with you." She snapped.

She started to cry.

"Don't." Taffy said raising her hand. What have I turned in to? She questioned herself.

"Madra." She said before being struck.

"That's better. Now get in the tub and after I scrub you clean, I will fix you something to eat."

"Why am I here?" Madra asked.

Taffy did not answer the question. Instead, she began to scrub off weeks of dirt and grime. She washed the tangled

19

hair. It was a very thorough cleaning. The bath made Madra's skin tender until she was dusted head to toe in some kind of powders that smelled sweet. Then she had to sit very still while her hair was combed and dried. It was left in her natural straight style but Taffy clipped the ends. She did get one curl which kept falling in front of her face. Next, she was put into all new clothes. A pink dress and ribbon were put on her. She got new white socks with pink trim and sneakers. She was told she would get to keep them.

She was given some macaroni and cheese, a glass of milk and a small candy bar, then led to a small room and allowed to watch television. The old cartoons would have made her giggle if she had not been so frightened. She finished off the candy and her milk. Taffy produced a toothbrush and toothpaste for her to use then left the room. That was the last time Madra saw her that night.

There was a large mirror on one wall of the little room. She looked at herself during commercials. She could walk up close and look at her hair or stand across the room and twirl in her new dress. She was almost calm now but still very nervous over why she was there in the first place.

On the other side of the mirror, Trunk and Matte watched the playfulness of the little girl. Matte fidgeted as he watched the little girl acting her age without knowing he was watching her. Trunk saw that he was pleased and popped the question.

"You have something for me?"

Absentmindedly, Matte handed over an envelope filled with paper money. Trunk counted it and put the package in his inside coat pocket.

"I'll pick you up at ten a.m. day after tomorrow. I have someone in the building, so don't leave me a dead body to get rid of." Trunk said without any hint of a smile.

"Right." Matte said. "When do I meet her?"

"Now." Trunk led him out of the room and to the next door. He unlocked the door and stepped out of sight for him to enter, then locked the door behind him.

Madra's eyes got big as she looked up at yet another stranger that had invaded her world. He wore a business suit and had a pleasant smile. He pulled a child's watch he had bought at the airport from his pocket. Madra took the offered gift timidly. Matte opened his briefcase and took out a bottle of wine and two glasses. He poured.

"Here have a glass of grape juice." He said.

"It says wine on the bottle." Madra told him.

"Wine is made from grapes. Aren't you a smart one?"

"Yes." She said. Then she took the grape juice.

Trunk was there at ten O'clock sharp. He knocked on the door and told Matte it was time to go to the airport. He left the room looking back at the girl lying on the bed. He smiled. Trunk did not smile back and drove him to the airport without a word. Matte tried to make small talk but after getting only a grunt from the muscular man, he clammed up and looked out the window. Soon, he would be home with his loving family.

Taffy picked the girl up off the bed and took her directly to the bath tub where she let her soak in bubble bath and cry until she got it all cried out. She found her clothes, replaced the torn garments and laid them out for Madra to put on. After two hours, she gave the little girl ten dollars and let her out a side door. Madra found a dry corner in an abandoned warehouse, there she went back to sleep.

Chapter 4

Madra hid the best she could at night. During the day she looked for food. Some people gave her their pocket change, occasionally a greenback would be given her. She smiled her best smile then, as she craned her neck toward the face of the stranger. The stranger seldom smiled back but would mumble some words that Madra never quite got. Something like, 'Bless you child' or 'You should be in school' or 'You should be at home with your mother'. Well, she did hear some of them but they were foreign words to her. She got the word 'bless' but in her limited world, a coin, a hot burger or a safe corner to sleep in were her blessings. She did not know but most would have considered those limited things a curse.

She was snatched from her sleep many times in the months that followed. The big man with the coat came only once a year to take her to the room with the cartoons. The man in the business suit stayed all night and the next day and night with her. He was rough with her and she always left out the back door feeling sick and sore. She still looked like the little girl who drank grape juice that first night but inside she was battle strong and street wise. She did not fight him or push him away as she did on the first night. He still hurt her but he did not beat her if she was 'good'. On these occasions she got enough money to eat hot food for a week and she always came away with a new outfit. She learned his name was

Matte. She did not like these times but they were better than other times.

Sometimes she would be sleeping when some man came upon her suddenly and raped her in the dark. She did not see the faces of these men but there were other things she remembered. She remembered their breath which often smelled like the garbage cans at the back of the bars and the ash trays on the street corners. Though she had long stopped fighting back, some of them hit her any way. She tried her best to find a good hiding place to sleep but these adults were good at stalking. Her young mind could not outwit them every time.

The blessing that she was not aware of was that she did not catch some disease. The streets were a breeding ground for HIV/Aids and other sexually transmitted diseases but she was not aware of them and could not have comprehended such a phrase anyway. She knew she was used but she was surviving.

Madra was twelve and had been having 'woman problems' for only a few months. She had heard the old women talk. She was becoming street wise. They always passed and so like other things she had to deal with, she dealt with this new thing. She was caught between being a little girl and a young woman now. Her features had changed. She could walk like the women in the short skirts when she wanted to.

The big man came one rainy night and took her to the cartoon room. She still watched the funny characters but they were not as funny as they once were. Madra knew what awaited her. She resolved to get through it and wear a new outfit for a while. She saved all of them but could not get in the first outfit she got. It was too tight in places.

Matte was not pleased with her but did the things he came to do.

"You look older." He said in a complaining voice.

"Yes." Madra said. "I'm smarter too."

Matte did not like the mature sound of her voice. He did

23

not like the absence of reluctance and fear. After this time, he would tell Trunk to find him a new girl. Taffy noticed the difference too. Madra did not have to be carried to the tub to get cleaned up. She did her own scrubbing and even smiled when she got her new things.

"Thank you Taffy." Madra said.

"You are welcome Madra. Be careful."

"I won't be back. Matte doesn't like me much."

"I know. You be careful." Taffy said at the door.

Madra thought she was eating way too much. Her tummy was stretching her new outfit after only a few months. She could not be growing that fast. It was spring when she visited Matte last. Now it was winter and she struggled to stay warm at night. During the days she found a place over the steam vents to stand but at night she had to get off the streets.

There was a lady who always passed by her on the street. One day, as it was snowing a little and the wind was cold, the lady stopped to put dollars in her bag. The lady also had a heavy down jacket which she put on Madra before she walked on down the street. It was the warmest she had been in winter, in her whole life. It was large enough to cover her bulging tummy and reached to her knees. She could wear it for years without growing out of it.

"You can sleep next to me." Madra was looking for a place to sleep in an abandoned building when she heard the voice. It was familiar. An old lady, who must have been on the street for a hundred years was talking to her. Madra knew her from previous days. She was nice and did not try to steal from her.

"Okay." Madra said.

"You been hurting any?" The woman asked.

"Some."

"Where?"

"My tummy."

"How long?"

"Since it started getting dark."

"You are going to have a baby tonight."

Madra did give birth that night. It was a girl. She named her Acelin. It was a name she had seen in a book found in one of the trash cans.

"That's a nice name." The old lady said. Now exhausted as was Madra.

"It means noble." Madra said proudly.

"I hope she lives up to that name. There ain't much noble about living on the street."

"She will. I just know she will."

Madra took one arm out of her warm coat and laid the baby there. In the morning light, she fashioned some clothes for the baby from the outfit that was too small for her.

"I have to work harder now. You will need things." She told the baby girl as she nursed it.

After she could move around and the old lady had stopped waiting on her, she went back to the street with her little bundle under her arm. Many times, when it was warm enough, she would lay Acelin in the big coat beside her. Passersby shook their head but placed a little extra in her bag. Some even went to the fast food place and brought back hot sandwichs and stuff. It was as if she were almost adopted by the people on the street but no one took her home.

By chance, she saw Taffy on the street one day. Taffy was all dressed up and pranced along the street causing men to stop and stare. She saw Madra an her new baby and stopped to see it.

"How are you Madra?" Taffy asked.

"Fine Miss Taffy. Me and my baby are fine." She said.

Taffy turned away and wiped at her face. 'Now where did that come from?' She thought. She had not cried in years.

Taffy walked away but was back in a few minutes pushing a baby carriage with a hood on it.

"You can't carry her all the time. You'll hurt your arm."

"Thanks Miss Taffy." And she was gone. She did not walk down that street again. The pain was too much.

25

Acelin slept on her mother's coat. Madra made do with what ever she could find to wrap up in. Acelin had gotten to big for both of them to get in the coat. The coat was not as beautiful as it was on the day she got it but it was still warm and cozy at night. Acelin would curl up and smile, then fall asleep almost immediately. Madra always tried to find a card board box to make them a little house. Sometimes there were none and the night air would make her shiver all through the night.

Madra matured and Acelin grew. Both of them were street wise now. Madra had purchased new outfits with short skirts and knit hose. When she got a date, she would hide Acelin for an hour and come 'home' with lots of money. Very soon, they would rent an apartment and have a real place to sleep.

In the meantime, Madra bought a few books. In the late evening, while they both snuggled in the warm coat, Madra taught her daughter to read. She taught her other things too. She could not afford to hold back 'adult things' from her dauthter. Madra knew full well that her daughter may be in the same situation she was in when she was young. *She was still young but could not think of herself as young.* She told her daughter details. She could not tell of the forgotten years before she was on the street. They were lost to her. Madra did tell her daughter about the strong man who put her under his coat and took her to a room with cartoons and about a man named Matte, her father.

"Your name is Acelin Street. Your father's name is Matte." She told her daughter over and over. She even wrote it on cloth with a marker and sewed it inside the sleeve of her coat.

Acelin was very bright. She had long straight hair like her mother. She had round big eyes that opened wide when she was afraid or when her mother told her one of the scary stories of the street. Acelin knew how to hide. She knew to avoid the police.

"Some of the police are good and some are bad. You can not tell which ones are good and which are bad. So, stay away from all of them, especially at night." She told her. "Hide and be very quiet when they are around. Stand near an adult if you see a cop coming. If they think you are alone, they might take you away."

Acelin's eyes got large. "Yes Mother." Madra hugged her tightly.

"I can't breath." Acelin said with her voice muffled by the big coat.

"I'm sorry. It is just that I love you so much. Someday we will take our money and go away from here and the street life. We will see what is outside the city." Madra told her.

"That will be fun." Acelin said. Then, she looked up with those big eyes and said. "Mother."

"Yes Acelin."

"I love you so much too."

Chapter 5

Trunk never took Madra into his stable. He would have liked to. She was a pretty girl. Taffy objected strongly. She could not take seeing those big eyes of hers and those of the baby Acelin. She knew her name because she had taken things to her from time to time. She did not tell Trunk she did it. It was just something she had to do.

If Taffy could have faced the situation, it would have been much safer for Madra working in Trunk's stable. He would not let anyone hurt his girls. The one exception was when he arranged for some business man to have a young girl to play with for a day or two. That was where his working capitol came from and so he made the exception. Otherwise, if any man got aggressive with one of his girls, it was he who went home and had to explain bruises. To the police, he was simply defending a defenseless lady on the street. They accepted the story. Once Trunk did get called in to answer questions but he knew many of the cops including the local chief. He had done 'favors' for them. They let him go.

Acelin was a whiz with numbers. She could count money with ease and remember street numbers. She had a knack for remembering dates too. She could recite all the important events of her life.

The night when she woke up and had to go pee and found her mother gone, she thought her mother must have gotten up for the same reason, so she followed toward the place they

28

used when staying where they were. She heard men's voices and hid like her mother had taught her. A police car was just over there in the darkness. Only the vehicles parking lights were on. She could make out one man standing with a flashlight shining toward the floor. He was laughing. Another man was on the floor with a wiggling form under him. The man ripped a garment off the wiggling form and tossed it aside. It was a dress. Acelin's eyes were very large now but she could not see who the wiggling form was. She thought for a moment that it could be her mother but her mother would stay away from the police. Acelin looked at the number on the police car and remembered it.

Madra had indeed gotten up to answer nature's call. She did not see the police car sitting in the dark until it was too late. The car started and blue lights flashed. She started to run back to her baby but decided it might be dangerous for the child. She instead ran the other way. The car cut her off. She was in a corner. A wall on each side and the police car directly in front of her. The two men got out smiling.

"Well, look what we caught."

"A real cutey." The other said.

Madra did not try to run now. They came at her on both sides. For no reason, one of them hit her with a baton on the side of the leg. She felt and heard something snap. She went down in an awkard position with her knees up. She tried to cover her underwear and hold her leg at the same time.

One was holding a flashlight and the other was doing something with his belt. She did not remember much after that. Both men took turns with her. She was numb to their actions. Once she turned her head and saw Acelin standing near, her white dress shining in the night. Just before the men were finished and one kicked her in the ribs, she turned to Acelin and mouthed the words.

"I love you. Hid." Then blackness, as a baton hit her head.

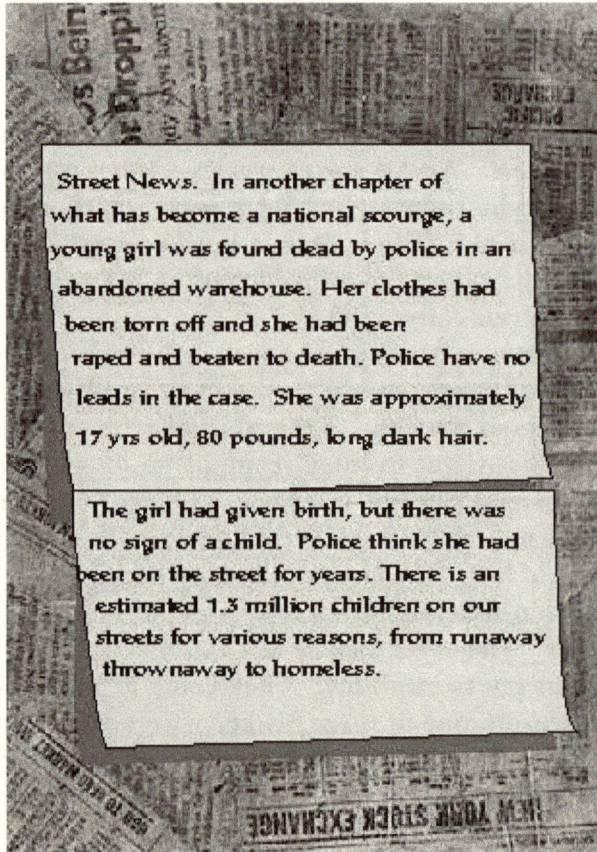

Street News. In another chapter of
what has become a national scourge, a
young girl was found dead by police in an
abandoned warehouse. Her clothes had
been torn off and she had been
raped and beaten to death. Police have no
leads in the case. She was approximately
17 yrs old, 80 pounds, long dark hair.

The girl had given birth, but there was
no sign of a child. Police think she had
been on the street for years. There is an
estimated 1.3 million children on our
streets for various reasons, from runaway
thrownaway to homeless.

Chapter 6

Acelin moved her stuff to another building. She climbed up dusty stairs to the top floor. There was a closet with a door in one room and she dragged her belongings inside. She spread her coat on the floor and curled up on the soft material. There were no tears but an awful pain filled her chest. As she fell asleep, she recited the phrase: November 21st, Mother died. Police hurt her then killed her. Car number 4671.

During the night she slept restlessly. She moved on her soft coat to get against her mother for warmth and comfort but she could not find her. 'She must have had to go.' She thought in her daze of sleep. In the morning, she sat on the coat shivering. The events of the night before came back to her and a tear rolled off her face. Through quivering lips she recited things her mother had taught her: My name is Acelin. It means noble. My last name is Street. My father's name is Matte. Matte used to hurt Mother. Stay away from the police. Stand near an adult if you see one coming so they won't take you away. Then another phrase came to her mind: Find Taffy. She is our friend.

Acelin pulled the coat tight around her and she was warm again but she still shook. Her eyes were very large in the darkness of the closet. Something moved near her and she whacked it with her shoe. Her mother said she was very smart. In a little while, she decided, she would go to their place on the street. Perhaps, the old lady would come by and leave her some money or food. Taffy might even come by. "I am very smart. My mother said so. I know what to do."

She stood near the steam vent, to stay warm, and held out her bag. She never knew if people would put in money or food. Sometimes a mean person would put their trash in the bag and laugh as they walked away.

A woman stopped and put a warm biscuit with sausage in it into Acelin's hand. She waited for Acelin to take a bite and then handed her a cup with hot chocolate in it.

"Don't burn yourself. You might have to blow on it." The woman said. She had a sweet voice. She did not stand real close to Acelin but maybe a few feet away. Most people just kept on walking but this nice lady just stood there looking all around and watching Acelin at the same time.

"Here. I'll hold your chocolate while you eat some more." She reached out her hand and waited for Acelin to hand her the cup. Acelin did not want to let it go at first but she needed both hands to eat the biscuit. Reluctantly, she handed over the cup and took several bites. Then she reached out her hand for the chocolate, not knowing if the stranger was playing a trick on her or not. The woman handed over the cup and still she did not leave.

"See that sign over there with the cross on it?" The woman asked.

"Yes. I haven't see it before." Acelin said.

"You are right. We just opened a place for people to eat and it does not cost anything. You can sleep there too if you like." The woman said.

"That's nice." Acelin said.

"You can come over at eleven O'clock for lunch. Can you tell time?" The woman said and asked.

"Yes. I can tell time. My mother said I was very bright. She died last night." Acelin said matter-a-factly. A tear fell off her face. The woman gave her a soft cloth to wipe her face with and to blow her nose.

"I'm so sorry." The woman said.

"It was the police, car number 4671, who killed her. They were on top of her and she could not get away. Then they beat her with their clubs and kicked her." The words just spilled out. The woman bent beside the child.

"May I hug you?" The woman asked.

"My mother always hugged me." Acelin said.

"Will it be alright if I hug you. I could use a hug myself."

"Well, if you need a hug, then I guess it will be alright."

It was a good hug. Both the woman and the child held on to each other letting some of the hurt spread from the child to the woman.

"You smell good." Acelin said after the hug was over and they both wiped away tears.

"That is a very nice coat." The woman said. She was in no hurry to move. A few people reached around her and placed some item in Acelin's bag. A little change, sometimes a candy bar.

"It is Mother's coat. I guess it is mine now." Acelin told her.

"Can I give you some advice?" The woman asked.

"You mean like something to remember?" Acelin asked.

"Yes."

"Okay."

"Don't tell anyone else on the street about how your mother died. The police might get mad if people know. They might take you away." The woman said.

"Okay. If you say so." Acelin answered.

"See you at eleven if you can take a break from your work."

"You didn't say begging. That was nice."

"Well, we all have to work to eat."

"See you at eleven then." Acelin said.

Charis walked straight back to the mission. She had intended to work the streets until time to serve the noon meal but her first encounter with a street child had been all she could handle. She walked past the volunteer workers and into a back room where she kept a diary of her missionary work. Her preacher husband found her there with her hands to her face. She shuttered all over and he knew his wife was really upset over something. Street mission work caused a lot of pain that must be cast on the Lord. He knew his wife knew that as well as he but still it hurt to see the children hungry and cold and begging for bread.

He placed a hand on her shoulder then knelt beside her and stayed there in silent prayer until she no longer shook. Then she told him about Acelin.

Charis watched the door as she served the hot food to dirty and anxious people of all ages. She noticed a variety of smells as they passed, not the least of which was alcohol. Many of the people used alcohol as a means to dull the pain of their every day life. They hoped to offer them another way to deal with the pain but first they needed food and a while to rest.

Finally, she looked toward the door and saw her. A bedraggled little girl. She wore a down coat that hung below her knees. A bag bulging with this and that, from her morning of begging, hung protected on her arm. She did not move to get in line. She just stood there to one side of the door looking around with those big round eyes. The little girls eyes went from person to person, sizing them up as danger or not. Her eyes went from tray to tray looking at the food. She, unconsciously, licked her lips. Her stomach growled a familiar sound.

A sound escaped Charis's throat but she quickly composed herself and walked over to the little girl smiling at this one and that one as she passed them. She saved her best smile for Acelin.

"You came. Are you hungry?" Charis asked her.

"Yes ma'am." She said politely.

"Well, so am I. Would you join me for lunch?" Charis could not help it. She gave a little curtsy. "I have a table in back where it is not so crowded."

Acelin did her own little curtsy and smiled. She and her

34

mother had little tea parties sometimes. They would act out some of the characters in the books they read together. The smile disappeared at the memory.

"To the kitchen, then." Charis said and marched in that direction. She looked back to see Acelin copying her march movements.

They continued the little story book game to the table Charis had hoped all morning they would use. Her husband smiled as he went out to take her place on the serving line.

"What would malady have today? We have soup and soup." Charis said.

"I believe I will have soup." Acelin replied.

"Good choice. Malady is very wise. I will see what else I can find out there."

"And smart too. My mother says...said I was real smart."

Charis did not dare reply. She took a tray and bowl to the serving line and scooped a generous helping. Besides soup and soup they had some greens, mashed potatoes and tea. But for Acelin, Charis went to their refrigerator and got a large glass of whole milk.

As they say in the story books, it was a grand meal with fine conversation and good company. Charis fought to hold back tears at every turn. When she did not trust herself to talk she would take a big bite of food and smile with her lips pressed tightly together. She saw the tention go out of Acelin as she relaxed in her chair. She ate fast at first thinking the food might be taken away and that this was all just a mean trick. But then after a while, she slowed down and mimicked Charis by trying to hold her spoon properly and wipe her lips when they needed it.

Acelin joyfully took a bath in the big tub upstairs. She soaked for an hour. Charis found her an outfit that was clean and fit her well. Acelin would not let the coat out of her sight so Charis washed it under her watchful eyes.

When those things were done, Acelin quietly gathered up her things and started toward downstairs and the door.

"Are you leaving?" Charis asked dreading the answer.

"I have to get back to my place. Mother said we should not be lazy and play all day." She said.

"I agree with your mother. Will you come back for the evening meal?"

"Yes. If it is okay. Mother said we should not be greedy."

"I'm inviting you. That would not be greedy."

"Okay then. I will see you after work." Then she was off to her place on the street.

Charis tried to make up for the time she had spent with Acelin but her husband reminded her of the value of one soul, so she went about her work in a normal manner ever glancing toward the street.

Chapter 7

Trunk's real estate business had grown in spite of the fact that he used it primarily as a cover for his other, illegal business. He now owned several apartment buildings in his area of activity. They were dumps when he got them for a small investment. He invested more money and cleaned them up, putting in new plumbing in the process. He dressed up the outside as well. Sitting in a somewhat rundown part of town, his buildings stood out from the rest as a vast improvement for the community. He was hailed by leaders as a very civic minded young man.

He did not like drawing attention to himself but he was very careful. He trusted his memory and wrote little down. On occasion he made a note for Taffy so she could adjust her books. The tax people liked good bookkeeping. He did not intend to be like the famous mobster and get hauled in for tax invasion because they could get no evidence otherwise. He did not intend to get hauled in for anything.

Taffy was also very careful. She faithfully kept her records on both businesses. One set of books had the company name, *Trunk's Real Estate,* on all the documents. The other set of books had no names at all. Numbers were used with only Trunk and herself knowing the names that went with the numbers. Both of them had the names and corresponding numbers memorized. The flaw for Trunk was that Taffy was an excellent bookkeeper. She made everything in duplicate and stowed away the extra copy in a safety deposit box. Her key was well hidden as well. She kept it in an envelope addressed to a good friend of hers. If she felt she was in any danger from Trunk, she would mail it along with its letter of instructions. It was just insurance and Taffy did not think she would ever need it.

Taffy met Charis on one of her mission trips to the street. She invited Charis to a snack and coffee in a local bar near where they were. Taffy just wanted to get off the street and out of sight of prying eyes.

"I do not socialize in bars." Charis told her flatly.

"I'm not inviting you for drinks." Taffy said just as flatly.

"Nevertheless, it is against my beliefs." Charis said.

"Okay. Okay. There is a little diner up the street. Will that satisfy your beliefs?" Taffy asked.

"That will be satisfactory." Charis replied.

They walked up the street together. The modestly dressed missionary and the swishing lady of many talents. Heads turned as they passed. Men stared at the flashy dressed one while others wondered at the strange combination. Both women were known on the street.

They ordered coffee and sat across from each other, making continuous eye contact. Two strong-willed women ready to hold their own in the conversation.

"I see you have made friends with Acelin." Taffy said.

"Yes. You know her?"

"I knew her mother." Taffy replied.

"Acelin is a sweetheart." Charis said.

"She is a time bomb waiting to go off." Taffy said.

"I don't see that in her."

"You don't know the streets well enough then."

"I'm learning."

"Acelin won't be around that long."

"What do you mean?" Charis asked, softer now.

"She is nearing the age when she will be a special prize for

38

some pervert with a pocket full of money." Taffy spat out.

"Sounds like you know something about that." Charis stated.

"This conversation is not about what I know. It is about a little girl who hasn't got a prayer." Taffy told her.

"She has at least one prayer a day that I know of."

Something happened in the conversation then. Taffy slumped a little in her seat. She took a drink of her coffee and then started the conversation back with a different tone.

"I want to help your mission." Taffy said.

"Because of Acelin?"

"Partly."

"I don't want to look a gift horse in the mouth but I have to ask about the rest of the reason." Charis said.

"I was alone once on the streets. I know how it feels to be hungry and to have no place to sleep."

"You survived."

"Did I?"

"There is hope for everyone." Charis told her.

"I suppose."

"No supposing. If you are breathing, there is hope."

"You really believe that don't you?"

"If I did not, I would not be a missionary on these streets."

"Well can I help or not?" Taffy thought of home for a moment and she did not want to go there.

"We cannot take any money earned by prostitution."

"Your beliefs?" Not so bitter now.

"Yep." Charis said.

"Okay. It will be legitimate money only. I do some book-keeping for a real estate man. I'll use that money." Taffy said.

"Sounds great. We can certainly use it."

"Can you look after Acelin?" Taffy asked.

"As best I can, we cannot force her. That would be kidnapping." Charis informed her.

"Fair enough." They shook hands.

"If you ever need to talk Taffy, you know where to find

me." Charis told her.

"Thank you. Where were you a few years ago?" Taffy asked, now liking the young spunky missionary.

"A few years ago, I was in high school and thinking my parents were nuts." Charis smiled.

"Yeah."

They parted then going their separate ways. Each week, the mission got a letter in the mail with a crisp hundred dollar bill inside. It was wrapped in paper but there was no note or explanation.

Chapter 8

Acelin kept a steady routine now. She changed where she slept every night. Often, she would end up back at the same place later. She felt like she was increasing her security but it was a routine that all the street people followed. They knew the good places where the police would leave them alone. The more affluent neighborhoods were off limits for sleeping but could be mined for a few dollars, if one was not aggressive. The aggressive ones would bring down the police and they would all have to scatter and avoid that street for a few days.

She was strolling down one of these busy streets when she say the little boy, of about three years old, just sitting on the sidewalk. It was early afternoon. Acelin had made her usual trip to the mission for the eleven O'clock meal and talked with Charis for a while after. She had her bath and was dressed in clean clothes. On this day, she did not carry her bag for begging with her. She looked so neat, she could have been mistaken for just another child waiting on the street for her parents.

People walked by the child as if they were going around some object left on the street by mistake. No one stopped to speak to the little boy or to ask him where his parents were. It was too common an occurance to be concerned about. Some parent probably just ran out of food in the house and dropped him on the street in a well-to-do neighborhood hoping for the best. Perhaps some rich folks would have pity on him and take him in. No one stopped.

Acelin walked down the street toward the boy and stopped in front of him. She reached out her hand and he took it. It was a little hand that reached out to him and because of their relatively same size, he sensed he could trust the hand. She pulled on the boys hand and he stood in front of her.

"Come off the sidewalk. We will talk."

"Okay." He said and walked timidly beside her. She pulled him from in front of the big people on the street. They walked very fast and must have had somewhere important to go. Some smiled at the two children, now, as they passed them. Such quiet little kids waiting for their parents.

"Look at me." He raised his eyes to her. They were wet with tears.

She took out a soft cloth Charis had given her and wiped the boys face.

"You need me to help you." She said.

"Mommy will come get me soon. I have to wait." He mumbled.

"I will wait with you for a while but I do not think your mommy will be back. What did she tell you?"

"She kept saying 'I'm sorry. I'm sorry.'" He told her.

"We will wait and see." Acelin sat with the little boy until it was getting close to time for the evening meal at the mission. His eyes darted up and down the street. People went on their way. From their point of view, it was pants legs and swishing skirts, shiny business shoes and clicking high heels. The car horns blew and people yelled and whistled for taxes. His mommy did not come. He started to cry.

"You have to stop that. I will explain all that later but you have to stop crying." She wiped his face again and gave him a piece of candy from her pocket. "We have to go. I know where we can eat."

"I'm hungry." He said.

"I know. I am too. We have to go. I'll hold your hand."

"What if Mommy comes?" He asked rubbing one eye with

the back of his hand.

"She won't come today. It is getting late. We will check again tomorrow." Acelin had seen it before. Children waiting expectantly for a parent to come back for them. They never did. The child would eventually wonder up and down the street and then crawl under a tree or close to a building and spend their first night on the street alone. Like having some sort of compass for street children, they migrated to the poor side of town. There they saw the other children begging for food and money and followed the example. They would get run off from many spots by bigger children before they found a safe place to 'earn their living'.

It was quite a long walk to the mission. The little boy was slow. He kept looking back, perhaps, expecting his mommy to come running down the street and scoop him up into her arms.

By the time they got to the mission, the door was closed and locked for the night. Acelin pressed her face against the glass of the front door. Charis had missed Acelin at the evening meal and was in a depressed mood. She worked on cleaning the tables but her heart was not in the work. She sat down at a table put her face in her hands. 'Where could she be?' 'Is she alright?' 'Could she be dead like so many others?' "No God please." She begged aloud.

Charis raised up and opened her eyes to see a little face pressed against the door apparently trying to see inside. She knocked over a chair getting to the door bringing her husband out into the cafeteria area. Charis opened the door and almost dragged the little girl into the mission. Acelin, for her part, hung onto the little hand she had been holding for miles. Both were inside and the door was closed before they could crane their heads to see who the big person was that snatched them off the street.

"What happened? I was so worried. Are you alright?"

Acelin's eyes were wide but she did not speak right away. She was shocked at the outpouring of concern. It was rare on the streets. Everyone pretty much took care of themselves.

Finally she spoke. "I'm okay. I brought a friend. His mommy did not come back." She said. Still clinging to the little boy as Charis had seen her do with her few possessions.

"Come to the back. I will find you some food."

Her husband already had the burner on and a pot of soup warming. She got some bowls and dug out some macaroni she was planning to heat up for their private supper. She got out the whole milk too. They had to mix powdered milk for the regular mission meals because of the expense. They had been trained to take care of themselves if they intended to be on the mission field for a long time. 'A sick missionary cannot help anyone.' They had been taught.

"What is your name?" Charis asked the little boy as she poured him a second glass of milk.

"Beau." He said. He had a milk mustache. Acelin reached over and wiped it away.

"You have to stay clean. It's a rule." She told him.

"It's a good rule. What is your last name?" Charis asked.

"Mommy calls me Beau. Just Beau." He said and ignored everyone while he ate the macaroni and soup.

Charis and her husband stood to one side while the children at their supper.

"They act just like children." She said without thinking.

"They are children. Acelin is a very old child inside but a child nonetheless."

"Of course they are." She corrected herself.

"You have to have your bath after you eat." Acelin told Beau.

"A bath!" He exclaimed.

"Now, don't be difficult." Acelin told him.

"I'm sor-wee for being dif-a-cud." He stammered.

"If your mommy does not come for you this week, you will be my brother and I will take care of you." Acelin told Beau plainly.

"Okay." He said. That won't be necessary, Mommy would

come tomorrow.

He did not think in those long words but it was how he felt. Acelin consented to stay in the mission for the night because of Beau. She just had to get up early to go check on Beau's mommy she told Charis. "I'm behind on my work too. I'll have to work really hard to make up for all this goofing off."

"Well, that's tomorrow, tonight you can sleep in a bed."

Beau's mommy did not come back for him. Truth is, she never used that street again until the day she died. Already she was expecting another child. A man had promised her he would live there and share his paycheck with her and the other children. He stayed for a month and left. How would she feed his child after the baby could no longer nurse?

Acelin began Beau's education. She told him about the street first. How to act. To stay clean. To stand by an adult when the cops came. He had trouble saying police. She showed him her secret places to sleep. Also about which people he could trust a little and which ones to stay away from. Then, she took out a book and started showing him letters. He did not even know what an 'A' was but Acelin was very patient with him. It turned out he was a quick study. She read to him when they were not working and told him to hid if EVER someone came and took her away.

"Go to the mission to eat when the sun starts to get high in the sky. Tell Charis someone took me and she will look after you." He looked very afraid when she told him that part but it was a necessary part of his education.

"Your name is Beau Street. You are my brother. My name is Acelin Street. My mother's name was Madra Street. My daddy's name is Matte. He was mean to my mother and hurt her real bad. My mother was killed by the police. Car 4671. It was on November 21st late at night while we were sleeping. My coat is very warm. It belonged to Mother so don't every loose it. You will forget all that but I will tell you again until you can remember." Acelin said.

"I will not forget." Beau said.

"Yes you will. Now, don't argue with me. I'm older." She said.

"Okay." Beau said and he never did again.

Chapter 9

It is somewhat of a mystery as to why Trunk did not feel more or any sympathy for the street children. He had, after all, come from the street and the exact circumstance as they did. It may be explained by the deeply rooted consensus that 'if I had to pay my dues to get ahead, then so do you.' It is true in the medical profession. A professor or senior doctor will not think much about pushing students and interns to the point of complete exhaustion as they try to make the grade. A brick mason will push the brick carriers until every fiber of their being is screaming in pain. The young cop gets the worst neighborhoods to patrol. So, perhaps, Trunk knew that the street child would either learn the ropes and survive or show weakness and die.

In spite of the fact that Trunk did not want to be in the limelight because of his shady activities, he was quite proud of his real estate ventures. This legal side of his business had given him status in the community. He was respected. Respect was something he had always won with his superior strength and a quick punch, when he roamed the streets. This respect was a different experience. He had lunch with community leaders and was viewed as one who promoted a better image for the city.

In that regard, real estate had become an addiction for him. He wanted more of it. His problem was that the upkeep of the properties and the salaries he paid out prevented him from having funds to take out of real estate to invest in new properties. Real estate was profitable but not quite enough to give him the amount of capitol he needed. He had hopes and dreams of 'buying up'. He had done okay by refurbishing the buildings in the old neighborhood but he wanted to move toward the more affluent side of town. The move would not be sudden yet he could buy property in that direction. There was a property for sale which with a little tender loving care could be turned into an upscale neighborhood. He needed more money.

That is how Trunk got into the movie business. He knew the internet was a gold mine for someone willing to exploit young boys and girls. The thought repulsed him but he did need the influx of some big money to upgrade his status. He did not want any part of the details. He wanted no trail leading back to him. for he knew that this was a big-time crime. The feds would be all over him if he got caught. His security cushion was to put up some money and peddle the flesh while letting someone else take the chances online.

Taffy started a third set of books. The copy she kept at their home office was all numbers and balance sheets. Her duplicate, however, contained the names that went with the numbers. She did not dwell on what might be happening in abandoned warehouses and never surfed the internet to see the result behind the names and numbers.

The lines in Taffy's face, around her eyes and the corners of her mouth, were premature. She still looked really good when she dressed up but inside she was scared to numbness.

She had all the time she wanted to herself. Trunk had moved on to younger girls by now. They still lived together and Taffy could either share the bed with them or sleep in a guest room they now had in their penthouse on top of their best property. She watched the girls pass through her house like people passing on the street. She cleaned them up if they needed it and told them to protect themselves if they would listen. Few listened. They were Trunk's girl. They loved each other. He had not lost his charm and good looks. He could get the older women or the young girls to fall all over their self to please him.

So, with her spare time, Taffy got her GED and went to college. She got her degree in general accounting and for no particular reason started taking courses in criminal justice. She was well educated now and it felt good. Taffy still played the submissive friend to Trunk. She did not talk about her education which far outreached the book knowledge Trunk had. She was his equal now and he did not have a clue.

Once a week Taffy went out with a lawyer friend from the other side of town. He knew her past and did not care. They never talked business and he knew nothing of what she knew about Trunk's business ventures. He was a friend more than a lawyer. He had cases and she had duties to Trunk but the twain never crossed, at least not yet. He sent some money to her elderly parents for her without asking why she did not do it herself.

Trunk received his once a year phone call from Matte. As a matter of routine, Trunk still watched the streets. He knew most of the sleeping places of the street children and what they wore. At least, he knew some item they would never be without. Something that held special meaning for them.

On this evening, he watched as Acelin came out of the mission with a little boy. Trunk did not know their names but he did remember the down coat that Acelin either always wore or had across her arm. It was her meaningful item.

It seemed it always rained when he had Matte for a client. He donned his full-length rain coat and went to the place where the two children slept. They would be fast asleep by now. The noise of the rain drowned out his movements in the old building. He thought as he went up the stairs that he might just buy this building and fix it up. It would, no doubt, raise the value on his other properties.

He approached the two figures who seemed to be fast asleep. He did not know that Acelin had been traumatized by her mother's murder and so laid awake for hours many nights. She did not move, unless she had to, so Beau would not be disturbed. She heard the foot steps of the big man and saw his silhouette in the faint light of a streetlight. Trunk was dumbfounded when she stood calmly to her feet and spoke to him.

"I know why you are here. Please don't wake the boy." She told him.

"Well, I'll be….." Trunk muttered.

"Perhaps." Acelin said but Trunk had no clue what she was talking about. He tucked her under his arm and the coat and carried her out to his shiny black car (a new one now) and put her in the trunk.

Taffy's job was easy but very sad. She recognized Acelin. It was different when it was not a stranger. She followed the usual procedure mechanically….numbly. There was little scrubbing to do. Acelin took most of her bath herself and sat quietly while she was doused with powders and her hair was fixed. Next, she got to pick out a new outfit right down to her skin. She asked if she could wear her own shoes. They were new a gift from the mission. She told Taffy. Taffy shuttered all over then, with the thought of the mission rushing in. She again shut down inside and finished the routine taking Acelin to the cartoon room.

Acelin sat watching the television with its funny characters and sometimes glancing at the big mirror. She checked her hair and twirled her new dress. Then, she walked right up to the mirror and looked at it as if she were seeing through a window glass.

"Can she see us?" Matte asked. "She looked right at me."

"Of course not. It's your imagination." Trunk told him. Then he said. "You know the drill, the money."

Matte handed over the envelope with the stack of bills.

Matte entered the room where Acelin sat. She looked up at him with her big eyes. Her long straight hair hung down her back except for the one strain Taffy had cut to hang near her face. Her lips quivered a little as he touched her hair.

"Do I know you?" He asked. It was a ridiculous question. Of course, he did not.

"No sir. We have never met." She said.

"Call me Matte."

"Okay." She replied sweetly.

Matte poured a few drinks and watched a string of cartoons. The little girl giggled a time or two in spite of her obvious nervousness. 'That was nice.' Matte thought. He was ready to go into the bedroom. He took her by the hand and she pulled away. He took her hand again with a tighter grip this time. She could not pull free. She finally relented and let him lead her into the other room. Her mother had told her about it but she did not say that.

Matte started getting undressed and she turned her head. He moved to get in her line of sight. He walked near to the bed and stroked her hair.

"You can take your shoes off." He told her.

"Okay. Don't hurt me. Please." She asked pleadingly.

Matte smiled and reached behind her. Acelin was not watching. She was pretending to take off her shoes but instead reached to the sole of her right shoe and removed a small razor blade.

"My mother told me about you Matte. You hurt her." With that bit of truth he started to straighten up to look at the girl again, then the pain hit him. His left leg was suddenly weak and he fell across the bed. The covers were already turning red. "You hurt my mother. I've been waiting for you." She said and knocked on the door.

Taffy came to the door and after taking one look at the bed pulled Acelin from the room.

"Children are solicited for sex, on average, within 72 hours of being on the street." ncfy.acf.hhs.gov

Street news. A man from out of town was found wandering the streets in the lower district. He was bleeding badly from his left leg. He said he had been mugged. His wallet was in his pocket. He seemed disoriented and confused.

Street news. Child porn is on the increase. Authorities find it difficult to pen down the culprits.

Chapter 10

Acelin and Beau stood at the door of the mission waiting for it to open. Charis spotted them and let them in early. She invited them to the back room to 'their' table. She was busy locking the door back and so did not notice Acelin's clothes until she got to the table and they turned around to face her.

"Acelin! You have blood on your dress. Are you alright?" She asked concerned.

"I am alright. The big man came to get me last night. I saw my father. When he started to hurt me, I cut him with my razor. He did not hurt me. I left. Taffy was there."

"Taffy? You know her?" She asked.

"My mother pointed at her one time. She said she was our friend."

"Some friend!" Charis said. Acelin did not respond.

"I'll get you children some breakfast. Are you sure you are both okay?"

"Yes ma'am." They said at the same time.

Charis was about the size of a big doll. She must have weighed ninety pounds. It was all bone, skin and muscle from handling the big pots in the kitchen. Her hair was red as a flame. She was told she had a temper but she just spoke real plain so people could understand her. Sometimes the words came out blunt but she was working on that.

She told her husband what happened and he was somber. She told him how mad she was with Taffy and he listened. "I intend to give her a piece of my mind when I see her, it seems she could use the contribution." Charis said out of hearing of the children. She was slicing carrots for the soup and was not paying much attention to where the slices went.

"That food would be better in the pot, don't you think?" He ask her.

She looked around her and at the floor. "Why did you not stop me before now?"

"Better the carrot than me, you little spitfire." He said.

She laughed. She had lost the battle with her hot head, again. He laughed with her and then told her.

"Acelin is safe. Right?"

"Yes. She is now."

"Who let her out of that place?"

"Taffy."

"Maybe, Taffy is the only reason Acelin is sitting here eating breakfast this morning. It is a bad business but Acelin is alive." He reasoned.

"Yes. She IS alive. I am sorry I was so mean. Hope. Right?"

"Hope."

Charis went to the children and got them more food and milk.

"We will be too fat to work." Acelin complained with a smile.

"Speak for yourself Sister." Beau chimed in. He was growing very fast. They all laughed at his sudden boldness.

"You will sleep here at the mission for a few nights. I want no arguments." Charis said flatly.

The children looked at each other and then back at Charis.

"Yes ma'am." They said together.

"Good. Now, Acelin you need another dress. Beau you stay and finish your breakfast." It was a new tone but they accepted it without question.

Chapter 11

The children were becoming a nuisance, a word the mayor translated into the phrase 'great tragedy' for the city council. They had come under fire from children's rights groups and concerned citizens of status, as not doing enough to help the children and clean up the streets. It was unclear to him if they meant the children were making the streets dirty and that getting them off the streets would make the streets clean.

The mayor knew the real filth were the people who used the children for their own pleasure but he did not say so. He also knew that certain members of the council had close ties with a supposed leader of the community. He knew about how much a man could expect to make being in real estate in a slum area. The supposed community leader referred to by the council member had other sources of capitol. He knew it, not from suspicion but from actual reports from the lower city. A time would come when he would expose the truth but today was not that day.

After the council meeting, the mayor had a sit-down session with the police chief. He did not like the chief but it was part of his job to keep the chief informed of the council's wishes. The chief nodded and puffed on a big Cuban cigar. Those things were expensive. The chief also owned a nice boat.

"The council is all up-in-arms over the street children. That street mission has the right idea. They keep them fed so they are not uptown bothering the nice people around city hall. Actually, the missionaries just care about helping the children but it is efforts like that, that do the most good." The mayor told the chief.

"That area is infested with crime. We get calls all the time and there is a stack of unsolved murders. Those kids are a pain." The chief stated.

"They're children. They cannot help it if their parents threw them away." The mayor suggested.

"Well, we got a bunch of runaways too. They ought to stay home and do their chores." The chief continued.

"I agree they need a home. You know though, many of them were abused at home and had no choice but to get out or be killed." The mayor explained.

"A little discipline never hurt nobody." The chief blew out a long puff of cigar smoke across the mayors desk. The mayor held his breath for a minute then responded.

"Chief, you and I both know, there is a lot of difference between discipline and abuse."

"Well, we'll work on it." Another puff of smoke. "I'll put my best men down there and see what can be done."

The chief got up and left the office. The mayor may have had something else to say but it did not matter to the chief. He ran his own show and everybody knew it.

Actually, for the next week, the chief diverted all regular patrols to the so called slum area or lower side away from that area. He instead took charge of the situation personally. A black van was used from the impound yard. Three burly cops dressed all in black, scoured the usual hiding places of the street children. One by one they found the children as they curled up on what ever they could find to sleep on. They were tossed in sacks made of black cloth. The chief stayed in the van and received the children as they were tossed inside. To stop the crying and screaming he simply hit them on the head. The first night a bundle of six children lay quietly on the van's floor. The chief lit a cigar.

"Here's you another one Chief." A calloused voice said.

"That's enough for tonight. It will take us another thirty minutes to dump our load." He said. "There's a movie coming on I want to see. We'll met again tomorrow night and work a different section."

A low chuckle went through the crowd of men dressed in black, their head hid with ski masks of the same color.

As the pulled up to the landfill, the chief produced a key. A man jumped out to open the gate. They could hear bulldozers working their way toward them to push the tons of trash over into low places. They would then cover the trash over with dirt to be hauled in during the night. All but the chief got out of the van as it pulled to the edge of the piles of trash. The husky men took a body at a time between two of them and tossed it over the trash. It would be at the bottom of the pile after the bulldozer did its job.

They tossed on the count of three. Each time they tried to beat their distance from the last throw. They droned as they worked.

"One for the money, two for the show and throw." Six times they sang the little made up tune.

"That last one kicked me in the face." One man said.

"You'll live. Can't mess up a face like that." They laughed.

The van was returned. The responsibility for the black suits belonged with the individual officers. They better find a good hiding place for them. The chief had told them.

Acelin tore at the end of the black material on the one end where she could see a little light. Her head hurt awfully bad. She managed to get her head out then one hand, then her shoulders. She slithered out of the bag and looked around at all the garbage. She had landed on a pile of bagged leaves. There were five other bags like the one she crawled out of. She started pulling the draw strings open and checking the contents. She could barely see but she felt them to see if they were warm. She knew how to find out if someone was alive. Death was a part of her world.

Acelin thought back to earlier that night. She and Beau

had found a good place to sleep. Charis had begged them to stay at the mission but for some reason, even Acelin did not understand, she was drawn to the street and the only life she had ever known.

Beau had punched her in the back. "I got to go." He said.

"You drink too much water before bed. It makes you go too much during the night." She scolded.

"I got to."

"Well go on. You are old enough to go alone. Just don't go too far. I'll stay awake and listen for you."

They both heard the van coming and the men walking toward them. Beau stayed where he was and hid. Acelin thought she was hid well but a pair of huge hands grabbed her and before she knew it, she was upside down and it was totally dark. She ended up with one hand on top of her head. That was what saved her life.

The bulldozer was getting closer but still Acelin clawed at the black bags. The last one she checked had a warm body in it. She grabbed the other end of the bag and without being gentle or ceremonius, she dumped the child out of the bag. The bulldozer was very close now. She could see the blade raised high in the air.

"Ouch! That hurt!" The body said. It was a girl.

"I didn't hurt you. Hurry up. We have to get away from the trash pile." Acelin said.

"Why did you bring me here?" Still not moving.

"I didn't. Do you want to be covered with dirt."

"N-o-o-o-o-o!"

"Quit arguing and help me then. We have to run."

They did try to run and fell over a bag of trash. They got up and tried to run again. A car tire tangled their feet. Dirt was starting to tumble down like the leading edge of an avalanche. It covered them with dirt and trash. Acelin again clawed herself free and felt around for the other child. She heard a cry and dug there. Up popped a head and Acelin pulled out the rest.

"That hurt." The child yelled and started to whimper.

"Don't be a cry baby." The girl cried louder.

Acelin grabbed her by one hand and pulled and dragged her in a direction leading away from the big machine which threatened to bury them alive. She had no plan or particular direction, just away from that 'thing'. She ended up at a slanting bank of dry red dirt. She looked up. At the top was a high fence. She started to climb anyway, dragging the other child behind her. She slipped and fell and once tumbled back to the bottom but she got up and went at the hill again.

It took an hour to get to the fence. Exhausted, she lay down. The other child squeezed against her pinning her to the fence.

Morning came with loud noises of machinery digging, plowing and hauling. The monsters attacked the trash like a gang of dogs after one piece of meat. Why had she thought of dogs?

They came in a pack. Wild, vicious things snapping at each other and running in their direction. Acelin pushed the child away from her so she could get up. She looked around and saw a very small space under the fence where rain had washed the dirt away. The dogs started up the red dirt hill toward them. Some fell and got in the way of the others making them even wilder.

Acelin again had to virtually carry and drag the other child toward the hole. It was small but they might make it. She pushed the child into the space.

"Hurry." Acelin screamed. She was very frightened now.

"I tore my dress." The girl complained.

Acelin grabbed the fence with both hands and pushed the girl through with her feet. She rolled onto her back leaving room for Acelin to scramble through. A large dog tried to follow her but could not immediately get through. Small dogs tried to get around the big dog but it got them a sharp snap. They backed off.

Acelin saw a stack of old tires and some odds and ends

stacked nearby. She started dragging and throwing stuff into the spot. The other little girl finally started helping and after a short time they had the hole blocked. Acelin picked up a rock and chunked it at the dogs. One yelped. She threw more and the creatures headed back toward the trash dump after the big dog jumped at the fence a few times.

It was several miles back to the city. The road the cops had used was a back entrance so there was only occasional traffic. When a vehicle did come by, the driver ignored the children. It was a common thing to see kids around the trash site which was why they had built the fences.

That night they slept in a metal sewer pipe. Acelin hoped it did not rain on this night. They slept fitfully because of their hunger and thirst. There was a puddle below the sewer pipe and the next morning the other little girl started to bend down for a drink.

"Don't do that. The water is dirty. It will make you sick." Acelin scolded.

"How did you get so smart?" The girl asked.

"My mother taught me." Acelin said. "Let's go." She took the girl's hand and led her up the bank and down the road to the city.

Beau woke up alone. He came out of hiding after an hour of waiting. Acelin was no where around. He called for her softly but she was not there. He waited all day and ate their only candy bar for supper. He slept on 'Mother's Coat', as Acelin called it. He was warm but hungry. He did not get up to go to the bathroom until the next morning. Then he remembered the men and the black sacks. They had taken his sister.

He cried for a moment but then stopped. Acelin would not like for him to cry. From deep in his memory, he had a thought. 'Go to the mission if anything happens to me.' He gathered up their things. It was a load for him. He took care with Acelin's coat. She would want it when she got back. Then he walked slowly toward the mission.

Charis met him before he got across the street. She had missed them the day before and had been up all night praying and crying.

He poured out his story. Charis had her husband call the police but they offered little hope.

"Them kids do that all the time. Don't worry about it." He slammed the phone down in a rare show of anger.

Charis was a wreck by the end of the evening meal. She asked everyone who came in to eat if they had seen the child. No one had seen her all day or the day before. She did find out that there were rumors of men snatching children during the night. A mysterious black van with men dressed in black had shown up in the middle of the night. The next morning children were missing but their stuff was still there.

Charis feared the worst. She walked to the front of the mission and back to the kitchen. She went outside and down the street in both directions. Several times, she did this, but it was getting dark.

Then she saw them. Acelin was always clean and well kept but the little thing she saw coming down the street was ragged and dirty. She was almost dragging another child with her as she stubbornly put one foot in front of the other. Her face was smudged. Her hair a tangled mess. Even on this street, people stopped to watch them pass. Acelin's eyes were fixed straight ahead. She would not be hindered from reaching her goal.

"What a kid?" Charis thought, then took off toward them calling to Acelin, Beau and her husband all in the same breath. She somehow gathered up both children in her arms and headed back to the mission. They smelled of garbage but it was the sweetest smell Charis had ever smelled. Hope was still alive. When she got to the door, no one inside had heard her and she stopped momentarily trying to figure out how to open the door. She was not about to put either child down. An old man, his hair uncombed for weeks, his shoe laces undone and his coat torn, opened the door and stood to one side with a toothless smile on his face. Charis stopped and turned.

"Thank you Sir." She said. He blushed and turned away. He was not accustomed to that kind of respect.

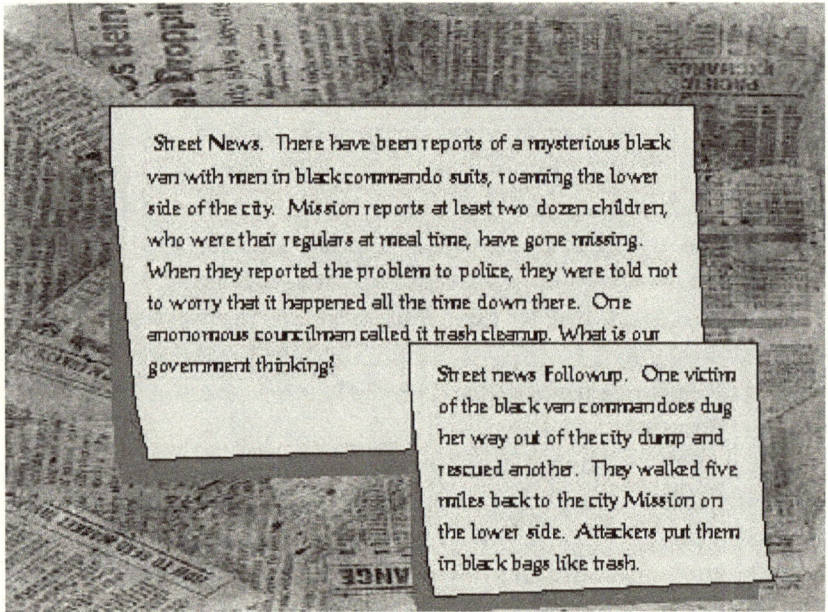

Street News. There have been reports of a mysterious black van with men in black commando suits, roaming the lower side of the city. Mission reports at least two dozen children, who were their regulars at meal time, have gone missing. When they reported the problem to police, they were told not to worry that it happened all the time down there. One anonomous councilman called it trash cleanup. What is our government thinking!

Street news Followup. One victim of the black van commandoes dug her way out of the city dump and rescued another. They walked five miles back to the city Mission on the lower side. Attackers put them in black bags like trash.

Brazil. A UN Human Rights report states that street children are often viewed as little more than vermin, and thousands have been murdered in the 1990s by police officers who see it as no more than a form of 'social cleansing.' J. Long. gordonconwell.edu

Chapter 12

A smart-mouthed young man came into the mission for the evening meal. He dangled a cigarette from the corner of his mouth and spoke very loudly. He walked directly to the tray area and started picking up utensils. The preacher, Daniel, came from behind the counter.

"You'll have to put the cigarette outside. It is against our rules to smoke inside." Daniel said.

"I ain't got much use for your rules." The young man said.

"What is your name young man?" Daniel asked.

"Everybody calls me Blade." The young man said.

"Well, Blade, you need to go outside and put your smoke out and then you can come back inside. You have to start at the end of the line and take your turn. That's another rule." Daniel told him.

Blade ignored the preacher and continued picking up his spoon, fork and other things. He then faced toward the food and smiled around the room. Daniel stepped in front of the young man.

"We are serious about our rules." He said.

Blade reached into his pocket and immediately everyone in the room knew why he was called Blade. Charis screamed. A movement of bodies, a pair of boots flying through the air and it was over. Daniel took the wrist of the hand with the knife and gave a hard twist as he turned his body. The knife dropped to the floor and Blade was pulled across the preacher's shoulders and onto the floor. Daniel still held the young man's hand and had placed his foot on the knife.

"I was saying. We are serious about our rules. Find your cigarette and take it outside. I'll keep the knife for you. If you still want something to eat, you may come back inside and wait at the end of the line. We are here to help but we are not partial to bullies." Daniel instructed him.

It was several minutes before everyone settled down. The food line started again and Charis dumped potatoes into held out trays. Daniel came to her side to help.

"Are you okay?" She asked him.

"Yeah. I used to do that stuff for fun. Hope I didn't hurt the fellow." Daniel said smiling down at her.

"Way to go preacher." Said an old man wearing a military shirt with sergeant strips on the sleeve.

"We just need to pray for him." Daniel said.

"And carry a big stick." The old timer said laughing. Daniel laughed too. He felt of the knife in his pocket. He well knew the boy could get another as easy as he had lost this one.

It took a week for the young man called Blade to return for the evening meal. He had a troop of various sized boys with him. It was a pack of determined looking boys.

"Today we eat when and where we like and smoke if we want to." Blade told Daniel.

Daniel tensed. "Call the police." He told Charis as he went around the counter.

"I can't let you do that. It would not be fair for the others."

"Who cares about fair. Me and my boys are hungry. They can wait." A knife came out from somewhere, then Daniel was aware of others flashing in the light of the room.

"The wolf and his whelps." Daniel said softly.

The police sergeant told Charis they would try to get a car there as soon as possible but there were none in the immediate area. She hung up the phone. Daniel crowded the gang a little leaving Charis room to get the children behind the serving line and into the kitchen. She was quick to understand that Daniel was putting his body between them and the gang and so she reacted quickly with some help from their regulars who scooped them up and followed her to the back area.

With room now, Daniel backed away pushing a table out of his way and maneuvering a couple of chairs with easy reach. He was a God-fearing man but he had no intention of letting a gang take over the mission.

Blade took a swing with his knife and heard his arm snap from a blow landed by Daniel. One knife down, how many to go. Blade backed away, holding his arm. Two more bigger boys came at him and he shoved a chair in their way. One could not stop in time and fell over it.

"Get him." Blade ordered as loud as he could holler.

"Stop" It was a new voice in the mix. Daniel kept his eyes on the boys searching for the most dangerous, those with the knives.

At the sound of the commanding voice, the boys scattered to the fringes of the room. Blade was really upset with them.

"I said get him." Blade yelled.

"Your troops are smarter than you are Blade. They know when to quit." A big man in a pin-striped suit stepped into the room and stopped directly in front of Daniel. Daniel had to look up a little to see his face which irritated him today with the mood he was in at the moment. Any other time it would not have mattered.

One follower of Blade started to obey his leader but never got past the big man. A fist casually slung over his shoulder sent the young man crashing into chairs and tables. He did not move again until his buddies carried him out.

"We come down here to claim this turf for ourselves." Blade finally addressed the big man.

"This turf has already been claimed and for some time now. The turf you are standing on belongs to the preacher here. What do you mean attacking a preacher anyway? Didn't your mother tell you nothing?" It was the big man called Trunk. He was not a nice person but he had his own code that he lived by. He might push his people a little but he would not, under any circumstances, let some upstart come into his area and take over.

"We just wanted to eat." Blade protested.

"Why, I'm sure that is alright with the preacher. He has a few rules but I've heard the food is good." Trunk said.

"Okay." Blade said. "What's the rules?"

"I'm sure he told you. Good manners mostly. No smoking in here it ain't good for the kids. Now pick up your boy there and straighten up this place. After you eat, you might want to get that arm looked after." Trunk said.

That was the only time they had any trouble with gangs. The boys lost their attitude and straightened up the tables and chairs. Then they politely lined up, making sure they were behind everyone else in the place. Trunk kept a watchful eye until all that was done. He then looked at the preacher and gave a slight salute.

"All yours Preach." He said and walked out. His eyes roamed over the once unruly boys.

"How did you know?" Daniel asked.

"I have people on the street. They tell me about everything, including the good work you are doing." Trunk said. "I heard about the tough little girl digging out of the dump too. Who did it do you know?"

"She only heard one name, or sort of a name. Someone was called Chief. They used clubs to hit them. That is all I know." Daniel said.

"Thanks. I'll handle it." Trunk said and he was gone.

Chapter 13

After a week, the 'street cleanup' stopped. The police chief had experienced a brutal beating in his driveway. He had no description of the culprits or their vehicle. He told the media that it must have been some excon holding a grudge. His three thugs were also random victims of violence. They told interviewers of their long tenure with the police force and the obvious truth that they had put a lot of bad guys away. It may have been an organized effort to teach the cops a lesson but all said they doubted that. 'Just part of the job.' They all said.

Taffy told her lawyer friend that she had heard rumors that the beatings were in response to the missing children from the lower city. Her friend did not further the rumor but thought privately that payday always comes. He had meet the chief and found him to be rude and unprofessional. He did not pursue the subject with Taffy.

For unexplained reasons and upon the advice of an unknown person, the council demoted the chief to captain and moved to a remote part of the city away from the lower side. His thugs were split up and transferred to undesirable precints in the city. The reason given for the actions was that the officers had failed to adjust to modern police procedures and misuse of impounded property. Their actions against the street children could not be proven and so the issue was not mentioned in their records. None ever worked the lower side again.

Taffy had advanced to a Master's Degree in accounting and was very close to that level in criminal justice. She had learned a lot about the nature of crime and had a deep understanding in regard to cause and effect. She and her lawyer friend often had long discussions about the law and the unwritten laws of daily law application. She learned that what the books said and the actual practices of the justice system were often far apart. 'It is not perfect. It is just how the system works.' Her friend told her and she understood.

Taffy applied for and received her Certified Public Accountant certification. She could now open an office when and if she wanted to do so. She had not yet decided what if anything she would do with all her education but she wanted to get out of the business of crime, hopefully without going to jail.

She talked about it with Trunk.

"I want to get out of the business." She said plainly.

"Why?" He asked.

"I have been true to your wishes for many years. It is a tough business and I am just tired." She said.

"You turning rat on me?" He asked.

"Have I ever done anything to hurt you?" She asked.

"No." He said. "Do what you want? Sunny can take your place."

"Let her go to school like you let me. There is a lot to keep up with." Taffy told him.

"You tell her. All I care about is getting the job done." Trunk told her.

That was how it ended. No farewell. No kiss. No last bottle of wine. Their trip down the back alleys of society was over.

Taffy had a talk with her lawyer friend who started the wheels turning for her paperwork with the city and state. She would have her CPA office after all. Her savings would carry her until her client list grew enough to support her. She decided to find a place with a residence upstairs so she would not have to commute. Taffy went to the mission to say goodbye to Charis and Acelin if she saw her.

"I'm getting out." She told Charis.

"I am so happy for you. You will be much happier." She replied. They were having coffee in the back of the mission.

"Charis. I have done a lot of harm I can never undo. How can I live with that and be happy?" Taffy asked.

"You ask for forgiveness. Forgive yourself, which is the hardest part. Then, you start over from where you are." Charis told her.

"Sounds easy."

"It's not. The Lord sometimes ask us to right the wrongs we are capable of righting." Charis said.

"How do I know which ones those are?"

"You will know when the time comes."

Acelin came in for a snack for her and Beau. She stood politely to one side waiting to be spoken to.

"Taffy is moving. You should say bye to her." Charis told her.

Acelin came to Taffy and clung to her neck for the longest time. She held no animosity toward the woman as Taffy could tell. Charis lowered her head and bit her lower lip to stave off the tears that were trying to escape. Taffy lost her battle with her tears and they flowed down her face and onto Acelin's shoulder. She raised her head and wiped at her face.

"I'm getting your coat wet. I am so sorry." She said.

"Mother said it was okay to cry if you really needed to but to not be a whiner. I can wash the coat. I will miss you Taffy." Acelin said very grown up.

"Shake hands with Miss Taffy." She told Beau. "She is moving away."

"Bye Miss Taffy." Beau said sticking out his hand. Taffy pulled him to her and hugged him but he pulled away, in typical little boy fashion, blinking his eyes.

Trunk, for his part, did miss Taffy but would never call her to say so. Sunny did well but never quite got the hang of keeping tabs on so many ventures and hiding them at the same time. Trunk yelled at her and cursed Taffy for leaving. He was still the picture of cool in public but grew bitter and impatient in private. The strain of knowing that he was only inches from being arrested wore on him constantly. He had too many people working for him and too many businesses to oversee closely, as he had in the early days. He feared that one of them would make a mistake that pointed back to him.

The part that gave him the most tension was not knowing where the crack in his empire would appear. He had done favors for many at city hall. Favors that they would not want to be made public. So, he was safe sofar as those men went. Still, someone might get too drunk to keep their mouth shut. Handling the most dangerous and critical enterprises on a personal basis might come back to bite him.

When these thoughts bombarded him, Trunk took another drink or two and changed his train of thought. His real estate holdings were substantial but still had to be propped up with illegal activities to make them the classy places he wanted them to be. He detested the idea that he might be called a slum lord.

At the mission, Charis and Daniel held school for some of the children. Charis had a teacher certificate and so did most of the teaching. Daniel had presented his supporting churches with the need for an orphanage. The response was enough to buy a small farm where the children could be taught to work and grow vegetables. Assistant missionaries came to help them at the mission. The school was moved to the farm. The mission became a doorway for the street children to what Daniel and Charis hoped was a better life.

The street children kept coming though. It seemed for every child that made it to the mission and out to the farm orphanage, two more would appear from no place. Daniel worked at the farm and at the mission. He walked the streets to announce the free meals. When they would listen, he spoke to them about a better Hope. As they adjusted, they were taken to the farm and shown around. Those who wanted to stay were allowed to do so.

Charis kept in touch with Taffy and in that way her lawyer friend. They sent out tracers to try to locate the parents of the children. Once the parents were found, if they were, a discreet investigation was undertaken to see if the parents were fit to care for their children. After a long and careful process, the children were either reunited or kept at the farm depending on the situation. The farm became a model for other missionaries and was praised by state officials. Taffy made sure the farm orphanage was properly registered to avoid any legal problems with the children.

PART II

"There's a special evil in the abuse and exploitation of the most innocent and vulnerable. The victims of (the) sex trade see little of life before they see the very worst of life, an underground of brutality and lonely fear. Those who create these victims and profit from their suffering must be severely punished. Those who patronize this industry debase themselves and deepen the misery of others."
President Bush, addressing the U.N. General Assembly.

Chapter 14

Trunk's Internet man had built a highly effective network for the distribution of child pornography. His many and innovative means to recruit the children were virtually endless. The process of indoctrination of the children into the porn industry was a step-by-step process. First, the child was found on the street and given the comforts they needed such as food and shelter. Those going along with the process were stepped up to the next level, those who did not were dumped back on the street or worse.

Next, it might be an innocent pool party where the actual abusers would intermingle with the children. Movies that progressively became more explicit would be shown. Then it progressed from there with seemingly innocent touching. All this served to 'soften up the stars' and reduce their inhibitions toward the next step. After all, they had seen it in the movies.

Finally, a fully equipped recreational vehicle or bus would take them cross country to some fun spot. It was on these trips that things became hardcore and the movies were made. The children now far from familiar surroundings were kept on a tight leash and for the most part were afraid to run. They, at least, knew their abusers. Only the most trusted were allowed to exit the vehicle for visits to theme parks or eating establishments but then with an escort.

On some occasions, the trip seemed like a family outing. There would be a driver who was employed by the business and a trusted prostitute would serve as the child's mother.

A special courier transported the finished product in a roundabout way to a safe country where distribution was made via the Internet using the latest technology and trickery. It was important for the business to stay ahead of law enforcement, so the best programmers they could find were used, sometimes at great expense.

Automatic systems were set up and file servers were currently being used for electronic distribution. Also known as f-serves. These servers provided twenty-four hour service, three-hundred and sixty-five days a year. It was impossible not to leave a trail at this point, although it was one hard to trace.

A more basic trick was to put a seemingly innocent looking website on a regular server with keywords and hidden text that would lead an unsuspecting surfer to a different website where any manner of child pornography would be listed with credit card payment forms and fees listed to go on to the next level. This bait and hook method had been used for years and was effective.

Trunk's man knew all the tricks. Trunk would not have approved of some of the videos he was making and did not enquire of the details. He simply laundried his cash payments through his real estate business. If Trunk had known the ages of some of the 'stars', he would probably have killed the man himself. The ages got lower and lower until five years old was common. Business was booming and the cash payments got larger.

Although the video guy traveled considerably, he also had a local operation where he made some of his videos. It was located in an underground section of a warehouse. The top floor was used to restore old cars. The mechanics were muscle men employed to watch the operation. They got paid in cash and in kind. Anyone seeing the place more than a couple of times would have realized that they worked on the same cars all the time and that there was no visible improvement in the appearance of the cars.

Acelin was ahead in her studies and so had an extra day to work in the mission. She had grown to a stunning fourteen years old and was quite independent. Beau had stayed behind at the farm to attend his regular classes. He was doing fine but could not miss classes.

She had spotted a bedraggled little girl holding the hand of a well dressed woman that may have been a prostitute. The little girl was not happy. The woman spoke to her as if she were the parent but something did not ring true to Acelin, so she followed at a discreet distance.

They were on the outskirts of town when the woman and little girl disappeared into a warehouse. She heard some cat calls and whistling inside but could not see anyone because she had to stay out of sight.

In an hour, the woman came out of the building and left in a car that was parked outside. It was a couple of hours until it would be dark. Acelin knew she should be on her way home but could not pull herself away. Charis was sure going to be mad when she did get home.

Finally, darkness came. Some cars left and the doors on the warehouse were closed. She went quietly to a side metal door with a glass reinforced top. She dared to look inside. She knew that anyone inside would be blinded to the outside by the lights that were on inside.

She looked around the area and saw a pile of debris against a wall not too far away. She went to it and soon found a stiff piece of flat plastic. She went back to the door and slid it into the crack between the door and its frame. Then, by pulling the plastic toward her she managed to slip the latch on the door. It was a knob locking door. She kept the plastic in case she needed it again.

By sneaking very carefully, she made her way to the far side of the building and found another locked door leading down a flight of stairs. Her heart raced but she was not about to give up on the little girl whom she sensed was in danger.

Opening the door in the same manner as the first she decended the stairs. No one was watching. Apparently, they felt secure in this isolated place.

Sneaking slowly and carefully, sometimes crawling, she made her way further into the darkness of the underground room. Now she could see lights ahead. She was careful not to stare at them and ruin her night vision, although she did not call it that.

Her eyes got very large when she came to a space between some boxes where she could see. She knew what a camera looked like and what a film making studio looked like from seeing them on television. That is exactly what she had found. This studio was very different. Acelin saw grown men and a very young girl on a bed together. Men and women stood around. Some were like coaches, others worked the cameras. She did not know what the others were doing.

Even more careful now, she made her way back to the stairs but on the way she spotted another door. The girl on the bed was not the one she had followed so she decided to go look for her. The other door lead to a short hall with two rooms off each side. Acelin listened at each door. At the last door, she heard a little girl crying. Again, she used her plastic piece and opened the door. There was the little girl she had followed from town. She was sitting alone on a small cot. She stopped crying when she saw Acelin.

Acelin took her hand and held her finger to her lips to tell her to be quiet. She retraced her way back to the stairs and up them to the warehouse. She took the girl to the door leading outside and pointed toward the debris pile.

"Go hide and wait for me. If anyone comes outside, be very quiet." She told her.

Acelin went back inside. She had seen an office in another corner of the building. She went inside and picked up the telephone dialing Charis' number.

"Where have you been young lady?" Charis scolded.

"Please listen. I need help." Acelin told her. She then told her the story of the little girl and the terrible things she had seen down in the basement of the warehouse.

"Go hide outside away from the building. I will get help. It will be there soon. I promise." Charis told her.

Charis told her to hide. She called Taffy who called her lawyer friend who called the FBI. They had learned not to trust the local police.

Acelin knew she should hide but there was still a little girl on that bed downstairs and it would take a while for help to come. Hoping the other little girl would stay hid, she went back down the stairs and took the same hidden route to her viewing place. The 'show' was still going on. The little girl was on the bed and a man was undressing her for the cameras. A man started toward her and Acelin could not let happen what was about to happen. She moved into the open.

"Why don't you try a woman and leave the kid alone?" She said boldly. She was little more than a child herself but she had been on the street a lifetime.

All eyes turned to her as she walked toward the bed. There was no movement at first. Everyone there seemed to be in shock at the new turn of events. Acelin prayed for precious minutes to pass so help would come.

"Go check up top." Someone said. That would be a couple of minutes. The man came back and announced an all clear.

"Why are you here?" A voice said.

'Good.' Acelin thought as she moved toward the child on the bed. She would answer that question and take up a few more minutes.

"I saw you take the little girl. She happened to be a friend of mine. I met her several weeks ago." A little lie. "She was hungry so I got her some food. Apparently, her family left her on the street because they were poor and could not afford to feed her, so I kept her with me and told her what she had to do to survive on the street. You see, I made a promise and I always keep my promises. I don't know what you are doing here with all these cameras but I think my little friend would be more comfortable with her clothes on and especially if I could take her home." So saying she covered the girl with a sheet and pulled her from the bed to the floor.

"You sure talk a lot." They were intrigued by this spunky intruder.

"Yes. Everybody tells me that I talk too much but it is what I do when I am nervous. All the cameras and lights make me nervous and I wish that big man would put his shirt back on. You all must be really embarrassed..." They cut her off.

"Really. You talk to much. So shut up and show us what you got." Acelin was really scared now. She had used up maybe ten minutes. She needed at least five more or ten. She started to undress herself. They watched.

"Keep the cameras rolling." The voice said.

"I'll teach you a thing or two." The shirtless man said.

Fortunately, Charis had taught Acelin how to dress as a lady should. She had on her coat, a blouse, an under blouse and so on. She used every minute she could to undo her buttons. She even fluffed her hair and bent her head over then back and moved her head around for the camera. She was running out of buttons and was down to stuff she did not want to take off. She moved around the bed in what she thought was seductive movement. She was faking the routine. The shirtless man lost patience and pushed her back on the bed.

"Here I'll help you with those things." He said. He reached behind her for her bra strap but stopped in mid-motion.

Acelin said very quietly so only he could hear. "The hand I have against your neck holds a very sharp razor blade. I have it against your carotid artery. Now, I might slip if I try to get from under you so you are going to stand up very carefully and pull me up with you. If I feel at all threatened, I will slice as deeply as my strength will let me. I am very strong for a girl. I will give you room to talk but only long enough for you to tell your friends to stay where they are."

Acclin told him.

"Don't move. She has a razor blade to my neck. Please don't move." The shirtless man begged the small crowd.

They stood up with the man pulling Acelin to her feet very gently. The little girl was crying now beside the bed. Then, finally, the time passed and men with guns burst through the door yelling for everyone to get on the floor.

"Don't shoot. I can't move. She has a razor to my neck." The shirtless man screamed.

"Good for her." An officer said. Then he carefully took Acelin by the wrist. "You can let him go now. We have him."

Acelin dropped her blade and ran to the child on the floor.

"They were going to rape this child. I had to do something. It is all on video if you need evidence. There is another child hid outside." She said.

"We will gather up everything. These people will go away for a very long time." The officer told her. "You may put your clothes back on now. It is all alright." He said gently.

Acelin had forgotten. She found and grabbed up her clothes then turned away to get dress.

Daniel and Charis were a few minutes behind and arrived as the officers herded a group of people into a van that had arrived soon after them.

Taffy and her friend were also there but stayed parked off to one side out of the way.

"I should stay in the car. I may know some of these people." He understood and did not object. He then went over to talk with the FBI.

"This is one brave young lady. She held off the whole crowd with a razor blade to protect that little girl." The senior agent told him. Then, Pete walked over to Daniel and Charis with Acelin and two children, both girls, in tow.

"They told me you could take these two to the farm. They will be out to question Acelin in the morning. It is okay if we leave now. They have a lot of investigating to do here tonight." He said.

"We don't even know your name." Daniel said.

"Pete. Peter Justice. Good name for a lawyer don't you think?" Pete said.

"Is Taffy here?" Charis asked.

"In the car. She thought it best."

"I suppose so. Tell her thank you."

"Will do." Pete told them over his shoulder. He left and they followed with the children. The one who had been on the bed cried all the way to the farm and into the night until she fell asleep. Apparently, Acelin had saved both the girls from a lot of trauma although being scared half to death was trauma enough. Just in case, they planned to take them to a doctor in the morning.

The FBI asked all of them to keep the whole thing quiet until they heard from them. They did not inform the local police department. The news media did not catch wind of the drama, that played out in the warehouse, until a couple of weeks later when the FBI announced that they had used the warehouse for a sting operation which had paid off big time. They now had the trail of those behind the child porn video operation. The servers were being confiscated and further leads were being developed. They promised they would chase every lead around the world, if necessary, to catch those who were profiting from the disgusting business.

'They are transported around the United States by a variety of means cars, buses, vans, trucks or planes and are often provided counterfeit identification to use in the event of arrest. Pimp-controlled commercial sexual exploitation of children is linked to escort and massage services, private dancing, drinking and photographic clubs, major sporting and recreational events, major cultural events, conventions and tourist

destinations. Estes Report. (CEOS) usdoj.gov

Street News. The FBI has released a report of a raid on a child porn operation in the local area. Using the location as a sting operation, they were successful in tracking down others involved.

Street News Followup. A young mission worker put her own life in peril when she rescued two children from the porn shop while waiting for FBI help.

Chapter 15

Pete Justice decided to run for district attorney. He was a quiet, methodical man. In the courtroom, he presented his cases with well-spoken but polite mannerisms. He kept his eyes on the person he talked to making them feel that they must tell him the truth. When speaking with the jury in his summations, each juror came away feeling as if they had had a personal conversation with the handsome lawyer.

His campaign was straightforward. He stated the district's problems with quiet resolve and clarity. 'It was time to eliminate corruption and the corruptors. The time has come for the parents of the children to step forward and take care of their children. Criminals who prey on our young people, whether in the home or on the street, must be put behind bars or run out of town.'

They were strong words that got the attention of many who operated outside the bounds of the law. Trunk had not been touched, yet, by the recent child porn investigation. He hoped he was well hidden behind the maze of deception he had put in place. Taffy could not turn him in because she had no evidence that would connect him and she would have to incriminate herself to point-the-finger at him. Those were the first two mistakes in his reasoning.

With Pete sure to win the election, she knew that her close friendship with him could bring him down because of her past. She decided to come clean with him then the district. She, at first, choose not to incriminate Trunk but only made public her personal involvement in criminal activities. Pete took her to the FBI where she was granted immunity for her disclosures about the methods used in the underground as it pertained to prostitution.

The details of her deal were not made public and so she came under suspicion by Trunk. He felt sure she had ratted on him and he intended that she never testify in court. The new district attorney was on his list as well. Trunk had never resorted to killing before. He had a unique ability to persuade people into doing what ever he wanted. His most prominent shortcoming, one he was not aware of, was that he had dealt with children and those who wish to abuse them. He had few dealings with people of conviction and integrity.

Consequently, he escalated his criminal mindset by plotting to get rid of Taffy. He sent a team to do just that. Trunk did not know that Taffy was much more valuable alive. He had no way of knowing that she had prepared duplicates of all his books, up to the time of her leaving, to be forwarded to authorities if she were suddenly killed. Her key to the safety deposit box containing the duplicates had long been mailed to her friend. She contacted her friend once a week to assure her that she was still alive. Her friend was reliable and would mail the key to the authorities if Taffy missed a week.

Pete Justice knew he was a target simply for the platform he had campaigned on. Those who knew him, knew that they were not idle words. Pete Justice would live by his promises to the district. First, in cooperation with the Federal Bureau of Investigation, he launched a very secret investigation of city officials and those connected with government. He had been around long enough to know which judges had been compromised.

Once an arrest was made, it was like dominos. They had to make a few deals with these first defendants to get to the next level of the investigation. The net widened as they slowly progressed in the investigation.

The Internal Revenue Service did a routine audit of all real estate companies in the area based on the testimony of one of the city council members. He said he thought at least one of the companies was laundrying money for the porn industry. He would not name names for fear of his life. So, the IRS in their thorough fashion, audited all of them. Trunk was invited to explain why his incoming revenue was much more than the revenue he received from rental income. He 'took the fifth' as instructed by his lawyer from out of town.

Because Pete knew he was a target, he planned his outings very carefully. He had a team of investigators who doubled as his bodyguards. It was when he took Taffy out for an evening meal that the attempted hit was carried out. Pete's bodyguards thought when it started that it was Pete who was in danger. He was in danger only because he was in the immediate proximity of Taffy. Taffy was hit by the first shot. It struck her in the shoulder and knocked her from her chair. She was conscious but being aware of the bodyguards, she lay very still. It showed remarkable presents of mind for someone who had just been shot but she had 'cut her teeth' in the rough streets.

The bodyguards attacked. They took a couple of body hits but none were killed due to their forethought of wearing vests. Pete blazed away with his own weapon and took down one of the assasins.

It was over in a couple of moments but it seemed much longer to the customers strawn on the floor trying to stay out of harms way. The hostess had already called 911 when Pete got his cellphone out. She told him so. The assasins were being checked for a pulse and their weapons rounded up. None of them made it and would not be able to tell Pete who sent them.

Later that night, after she was treated, her injury turned out to be rather minor, Taffy asked Pete if they could have a serious talk. Of course, he had said but didn't she need to rest first. It cannot wait, she had told him.

"I was the target tonight." She opened the conversation.

"I thought you might be or they were very bad shots."

"It was Trunk. He is afraid."

"What could he fear from you? You did not implicate him in anything."

"He does not know that."

"Right on that point."

"I was never angry with Trunk until tonight. He had no reason to send people to kill me. In fact, my death would have put him away for life. I have a good friend who holds the key, literally, to a lot of evidence against him. You see, we always used numbers instead of names. Trunk and I had the names memorized with the corresponding numbers. What Trunk does not know is that I was taught in accounting classes to always protect myself with duplicate books. In that manner, I could not be pulled into court and used as a scape-goat. I did make those duplicates and included the names."

Taffy rested from her speech which spilled out of her now that she had started. She had kept the secret so long.

"How many years?" Pete asked.

"From the time I was fourteen until I quit." She said.

"That is a lot of evidence." Pete said.

"Will my immunity hold with these new revelations?" Taffy asked.

"Yes. It was for any and all activities relating to your past activities." Pete said.

"Do you hate me now? Or will you hate me after you see all the stuff I did?" Taffy asked with a tear in her eye.

"Far from hate. I love you very much which brings me to the occasion of our evening out." He dug around in his pocket and came up with the little box. "Will you marry me."

"Yes." She said and cried outright.

Chapter 16

Acelin finally realized that she had outgrown the coat her mother gave her. It was sad in the respect that she had the life her mother would never know. Never knew in her short life. Acelin had outlived the years her mother had. Some of Acelin's life had been rough and dangerous but she had also known some good times, some safe times. Her mother never did have anything but struggle and danger.

Daniel made her a box with a glass front after she announced that she would put the coat away.

"We will make a place on the wall for your Mother's Coat." Charis said. "It has a story to tell. It makes me think of hope and why we do what we do."

A simple inscription was put at the bottom. Daniel had it made special on a brass plaque. It read: Mother's Coat.

Acelin worked the farm, the streets and went on to college. Her memories of the past had not gone away. She had many good memories since her early childhood but somehow things seemed unfinished. That awful night in the cartoon room came flooding back when she picked up a newspaper and saw Matte's picture on the front page.

The article was typical. It told of his years in private industry and then his stint in the state house. He went on to run for the United States Senate and had served the most part of a six year term. He was announcing his candidacy for President of the United States.

Acelin had let the hardness she developed as a street kid

slowly leave her being. She warmed to people easily and took her work with the mission very seriously. She sat now, staring at the picture on the front page. She sat very rigid and her eyes were set. She felt bitterness for the first time since she held the razor blade to the shirtless man's throat in the child porn studio. Charis came in the room and gently touched her on the shoulder. Acelin jumped from the chair and took on the stance of a wild animal.

"Acelin. What is the matter.?" Charis asked.

Acelin could only point. She tried to speak but the words would not come as her lips quivered. Charis approached her slowly and put her arm across her shoulders.

"Come sit down. I will make us some tea." Charis said.

Mechanically, Acelin sat down and stared at nothing.

Charis got the tea hot and brought it to the table. She sat and waited for Acelin to speak. It was sometime before she raised the cup of tea and took a small taste. Then, she lifted her eyes to Charis and pointed at the picture.

"He is from the cartoon room." Acelin said.

Charis picked up the paper and read the article. The man seemed to be the answer to the country's needs. He had the looks and the experience. His intentions seemed honorable.

"Are you sure?" Charis asked.

"Absolutely." I might forget my own face but never his." She said.

"I know it is upsetting for you but we must forgive and go forward. He is a vile man and we will just have to pray that he does not become our president." Charis reasoned.

"He raped my mother and is my father." Acelin said sadly.

Charis gasped. She had no immediate answer for that kind of pain. Acelin had never told her the whole story before.

"Mother made me remember him. She thought that I would have to face him someday and I did. I cut his leg very badly. He bleed a lot and I ran away." Acelin explained.

"I am so sorry." Charis said.

They watched the news on television that night, hoping to

get a glimpse of the man. They did get to see a replay of his announcement on a stage in his hometown. Unlike most of the candidates they had seen, who briskly walked up the steps and across the stage. This man climbed the steps slowly and walked across the stage with a pronounced limp. He made the initial announcement and then launched into his promises.

"As a victim of violent crime myself, I have a personal interest in cleaning up our streets. As a father and grandfather, I have a personal interest in making our streets safe for children. If I am elected president, I will make it my personal goal to seek out and see brought to justice those who prey on children for their perverted pleasure."

"The man has a lot of audacity to make a speech like that." Daniel said. Charis had told him the story.

"He must think he is well protected." Charis said.

"He will take the office of president as a license to do what ever atrocities he fells like." Daniel continued.

Acelin did not join in the conversation. She kept replaying the segment of the speech she had heard and remembering a long wet night when she was in the cartoon room and the other room. She saw his face on the television screen even after the program changed to something else. Daniel and Charis stopped debating the issue and looked toward Acelin. She had come so far since the streets. It would be a terrible thing for this to erase her progress.

She went to classes the next day and dropped a short note in the mail after surfing the Internet for Matte's website and address.

Matte was in full swing. He was working toward his parties nomination and was in New Hampshire full of energy and in the company of a senior senator. He had made the connection with the senator through the help of the man who had purchased his house long ago. They hit it off right away and had spent much leisure time together.

Matte did not see a lot of his campaign mail but his

campaign manager brought this short note to him after a speech where he again expounded the evils of sex trade and exploitation of America's young people.

"What's the deal?" Matte asked.

"This note sounds genuine. Could it be?" His manager asked. The note was very simple. It first asked a question.

Do you remember the cartoon room? I know the truth about how your leg got hurt. Stop your campaign.

Signed: Your Daughter

There was no return address and it was mailed from a college post office, so it could have come from any of several thousand college age students.

"Not one iota of truth to it. We expected this kind of thing. She is probably some college girl who wants a job in the White House." Matte said.

"You better be sure Senator. A lot of people have associated themselves with your campaign. Something like this could bring down the house on all of us."

"It is a lie. Now, you have work to do." Matte said.

After the campaign manager left the room, Matte took out a lighter and burned it in an ash tray. He had words for Acelin but they remained unspoken.

Matte made his way onto the stage. He had used his injury to further his career by coming out strong against crime but he would have much preferred to walk briskly to the podium. He looked out over the waving crowd. They surely loved him and what he stood far. The question in the note came to his mind as he was remembering the first line of his speech today. *"Do you remember...* He started off. He paused and smiled at the crowd as they replied. "Yes we remember." The mistake was on the evening news. The news people were vocal in wondering what it was the candidate wanted everyone to remember. No explaination was forthcoming.

The campaign manager kicked his foot on a post of the hastily constructed stage. 'It was true.' He said aloud.

They left the state for the next one on their long journey to what they believed and hoped would be the nomination. There was nothing, they knew of, that could stop them. They had the momentum and their closest competitor was far behind in the poles. Another note came from the college post office. It was equally short.

Do you remember my big round eyes and dark hair? I know who you paid the money to. Stop your campaign.

Signed: Your daughter

The campaign manager slammed the door rousing Matte from his note taking for his next speech.

"No iota of truth! That is what you said." He handed Matte the short note. Matte read it and looked up with the ease of one accustomed to lying with a straight face. He looked his campaign manager in the eyes.

"How long have you known me?" Matte asked.

"Twenty years." He said.

"You know my wife, my daughter and my grandchildren. You have been with me since the business days. Now, can't we ignore this kind of junk mail and concentrate on the real issues of the campaign. This is the White House we are talking about here." Matte told him firmly.

"Okay, okay. I have to warn you though. These notes have a ring of truth to them. Someone trying to make up a story would have been more long winded. We get one more note with new details and I am out. I mean it. You will have to get a new campaign manager." He said.

"Fair enough." Matte said.

Matte was getting into the swing of a national campaign. He worked the crowds and made speeches then jumped on his

90

chartcrcd planc and went to the next city. He was tired by the weekend though and intended to take a day off after his next speech. He mounted the stage. Every limp he made was a reminder to the crowd of how much this man must hate criminals and crime. He had good reason. The story was well known how he had fought with his attackers while one of them sliced his leg with a sharp knife. He started his speech in fine fashion. The crowd was certainly 'into it'.

"We are here today, not just to smile for the media and put on some kind of show. We are here today for the child standing next to some of you mothers and fathers. We are here for the children all over the country who find themselves in an abusive situation. We are here to represent the child who has no parent to throw a ball or have a pretend tea party. For those who sit alone watching cartoons....cartoons...ah...we are here for those who must deal with life's problems and stare at their own tears in the mirror...the mirror...of life."

Matte looked over the crowd as he stammered for the first time in a political speech. His mind kept going back to that room where he stood behind a mirror and paid money to a man with no last name so he could take liberties with a girl who was defenseless against him. As he gazed at the crowd, they looked at each other wondering why their candidate was not finishing his speech. Every child in the mass of people seemed to be magnified in his sight. He saw young girls with long, straight dark hair and big round frightened eyes.

"We are here for the children." He finally continued. The smiles came back the mass of faces. "We are here for every child, no matter what race, creed or religion. No matter if they have curly brown hair, wavey blone hair, bouncey auburn hair, or long straight hair....with big round eyes...ah...no matter what, we are here for the children. He finished quickly. His campaign manager kicked the stage post again.

The media had a feeding frenzy over the missteps. They played them over and over.

"He is like a robot with a glitch in its computer chip." One commentator said. He was reprimanded for it but the deed was done.

Matte took a few days off and mended some fences with his handlers. His campaign manager quit but he found another one and micro-managed the unexpected exit with the media.

"He had some family issues. We are still the best of friends and this is for his benefit. I will miss his compainship and advice greatly." So went the press release.

His speeches went well too. He was up in the polls and still far ahead of his challanger, even with the botched speeches. There was still plenty of time and the money was still coming.

The next note was not to Matte. It went to his wife.

Do you know what Matte's once a year withdrawals for several thousand dollars was for? He likes little street kids.

Signed: Matte's Other Daughter

Daria confronted Matte and he denied the whole sorted idea that he would stoop so low. He was dismayed that she would give even the slightest credence to the note. What if Deanna heard such things? Daria was properly scolded and dropped the subject. She hid the note where it would not be found.

Daria was a pretty good accountant in her own right. She went to the basement and dug through some old bank account files. She well remembered one of the years. Deanna was fourteen and they had sold one of their houses. That was when Matte had gone around her and let Deanna wear that low cut blouse underneath a more conservative one. Daria visited the school that day on another matter and saw her daughter. She was in a group of girls dressed in the same manner and several boys were feasting their eyes. The girls giggled their excitement. Daria watched more closely from then on but never mentioned the incident. Her daughter had not noticed her at school.

Daria found the file she was looking for. It was a seven thousand dollar withdrawal. She then moved to a box labeled for a year later. In about the same week timeframe, she found the second check. This one for eight thousand. They made good money and so the transaction was not noticed or must have been smoothed over by some casual comment. She wrote checks for charity and sometimes gave cash when it was more convenient, so Matte did not have to explain his every action to her.

She kept digging and found several more. Each one just under the ten thousand dollar limit that would have caused the government to ask for an explanation. She put the checks with the note in her secret hiding place.

Her husband wants to be president and he does not know that 'the chickens come home to roost'. She thought.

Trunk watched the news too. He saw the blunders of the man running for president and knew exactly what it all meant. 'The fool. Getting a guilt complex in front of millions of people. Next thing, he'd be calling his name.' He thought.

Trunk was waiting for trial and it did not look good. It was worse than he thought. Pete Justice held the duplicate books that Taffy had kept. Taffy was a good accountant. He used those books to get the ones Sunny was keeping for Trunk. By comparing both sets, any doctoring of the numbers would be obvious.

Trunk was indicted and was facing the rest of his life in prison. His assets were frozen and he had to rely on a public defender since his out of town lawyer would not defend him pro bono publico.

Pete Justice had an interview with Trunk before his arraignment on a multitude of charges.

"Here is the situation Trunk. You will be going to prison. There are a few things I can do for you in exchange for some information." Pete paused for a response.

"What things?" Trunk asked.

"Where you spend your prison time is one option. You know about doing, what is called, hard time and easy time. For the right information, I can arrange for you to be in a minimum security prison where you can pursue certain interest not related to the crimes you are charged with. I can also arrange for some years to be knocked off. For example, there are those who prey on the very young. You give me a name of one, I will give you five years for the information." Pete paused again.

"I can live with that. I never liked those kind of people in the first place. I just needed the money." Trunk said.

"I recommend you answer questions very specifically and do not elaborate. I am the district attorney and any information you give me that I do not have could be used against you in a court of law." Pete told him.

"Okay. I get it. Ask me a question?" Trunk said.

"Do you have memory of any specific individual who has preyed on young girls?" Pete asked.

"Yes." Trunk replied.

"What is their name?" Pete asked with pen in hand.

"The whole country has been looking at him every evening on the news." Trunk said.

"His name?" Pete asked.

"Matte Slither." Trunk told him.

"You have proof."

"Sure, I took a snapshot of him with the girl. I never told anyone. It was my insurance policy." Trunk said.

"Good. We will need all your snapshots." Pete said. It was a new source of evidence he had not expected. With the books that Taffy provided and the pictures. It was more than enough to win a case against Matte Slither.

"I have one small request." Trunk said.

"Yes."

"I'd like to see Slither's on television when he finds out you are going to arrest him." Trunk said smiling.

"That can be arranged." Pete smiled a little at the thought

of that. No honor among child abusers.

District Attorney Peter Justice made a special road trip to join the arresting officers who would pick up Matte. He did not intend to make it pleasant for him.

Matte was pumped for his next speech. He stood in front of the mirror in his bathroom going over his opening remarks and checking his suit.

Daria handed him several papers which were stapled in one corner and neatly folded.

"You might want to read this before you go on." She told him and walked away.

Matte opened the papers and began to read. He put the toilet lid down after the first line and sat down.

Daria Slithers v Matte Slithers

Notice: You are hereby notified that Daria Slithers has filed divorce proceedings against you, Matte Slithers, for diversion of mutually held funds from your joint accounts for the purpose of infidelity. In so doing, you are hereby further notified that you are in breach of the marriage contract. For this reason and other reasons which may come to light pending the investigation of the disbursement of said funds, Daria Silthers has made legal filing to sever your joint contract of marriage.

Further: All assets under the name of Daria Slithers and Matte Slithers and any unlisted accounts are hereby frozen until the case comes to trial and is ruled on by the courts. The courts will, in the mean time, provide living expenses from the accounts based on reasonable requests.

Additionally: Matte Slithers is to vacate the premises upon receipt of this notice. The court grants one hour to pack sufficient personal items for a one week period. All other properties will be disbursed in accordance with the court ruling at trial.

The attached documents are hereby made part of this notice and contain further clarification.

Under my hand this date: _____signed and dated _____

Matte packed his bag and went to the car. Daria was in the kitchen drinking coffee at the dining table. Matte glanced her way but did not speak or wave. Matte was thinking that she would regret this divorce when he was in the White House and people were bowing to his every wish. She would be left out of all of it. He felt sorry for her. He would invite Deanna to live in the White House. He just knew she would love it.

Daria received a courtesy call from Pete Justice as soon as he arrived in town. Daria listened, thanked the man, informed him of the divorce proceedings and hung up. She then called Deanna and told her the whole sorted story.

Matte listened to the crowd as they were prepped for his appearance on stage. Pete and the arresting officers were delayed by the local district attorney where Pete had to explain in detail that his case was airtight.

The local district attorney asked if they could delay until the speech was over. He did not want his friend the candidate to be embarrassed in public.

"Due to the nature of the crimes he is charged with, we wish to serve our federal warrants as soon as possible and transport the accused to the district where the crime was committed." Pete explained.

Matte walked onto stage. The crowd loved him. His leg hurt today and he limped more. His smile was as radiate as ever though. He flashed it for an extended period as he waved at the adoring crowd.

His security team turned to block the approaching men in suits but quickly moved aside after being shown the golden shields of the Federal Bureau of Investigation.

Matte quieted the crowd and began his speech. The agents approached from both sides. Peter walked behind two agents who would check the suspect for weapons and handcuff him.

"Ladies, Gentlemen and children of America. Many will not find our cause a just one. Those of us who respect and try to uphold the laws of our great nation must press on toward our goal. The vermin that threatens our security and the well being of our families must be stamped out. We must…."

Officers approached from both sides. Matte turned to the right then to the left. He wondered where his security detail had gotten off to.

"We must not rest until every back alley and every gutter is cleared of people who prey on the innocent and defenseless. It is our responsibility…."

The men were beside him now. He stammered but no words came out. He objected to the officers.

"What…what's going on? Do you know who I am?" The microphone was still turned on. Pete stepped near Matte and read from a paper in his hand.

"Matte Slithers, you are under arrest for abuse of a minor, to wit, a specific minor female in a specific location listed in documents that will be made available to you and your defense attorney upon request. You have the right to remain silent. Anything you say, can and will be used against you in a court of law. Officers please search and cuff the suspect. On a personal note, I agree that the vermin must be brought to justice."

The crowd stood in stunned silence. They had heard every word exchanged. They also saw Matte Slithers patted down and handcuffed. No doubt he would cry public humiliation as part of his defense but it would be pointed out that the local district attorney demanded an explanation before the arrest could be made which delayed their arrival to arrest Mister Slithers. In the end, it was one of his own friends who made the arrest a public event.

Television stations cut away from regular programming and went live. The feed was raw and uncut. The *world* was witness to the drama.

Chapter 17

Acelin changed her course of study to one in computer technology. She had a two fold purpose for doing so. She had a desire to understand how child porn was so easily put into the hands of the general public without more people being sent to jail. She also wanted to meet people that could be trusted and had the knowledge necessary to track down and destroy the means of producing and distributing such material.

She took a course in the legal aspects of the making of such materials, current laws concerning internet distribution and any means available of tracking the culprits.

The law, she found lacking. There were many loopholes through which the slime could creep to further their business. Hiding servers and money out of this country and using those countries which did not pursue criminals of this type were two ways they had of staying ahead of the law. Such things as freedom of speech rulings and personal privacy, though they must be considered, further hampered investigation by law enforcement agencies.

Upon finishing school, she had made friends with people who where at the top of their class in understanding the system and were people of high integrity. She made sure to keep their contact information and had personal meetings with them to explain her goals.

Next, Acelin had a long talk with Pete and Taffy. In order to do the kind of investigating she intended to do at the foundation, she needed clearance from the justice department else she would be singled out as a criminal instead of one who was trying to catch the criminal.

Pete was well connected and respected in the legal community. People, in high places, had hopes for him in the future although Pete did not yet see beyond cleaning up their district. He had made great headway but there was still work to do. Acelin, on the other hand, had international goals and aspirations. She intended to track the criminals around the globe if it meant getting one little girl or boy out of their grip and started on a normal life.

Acelin assembled her team. It included several lawyers around the country and some with international expertise who, through Pete, had promised to work with her when the need arose. She set up several fake accounts which if tracked would appear to be private residence. She purchased the best facial recognition software on the market. Known criminals, regardless of their specialty or location were fed into the database. Reports of missing children were uploaded. All unidentified remains of children and young adults were entered with known circumstances and locations. It was a massive undertaking and required many hours of computer work before they were ready to start the project. With Taffy's permission, she hired several reliable programmers for this task.

With safeguards in place and every contingency accounted for to conceal the true identity of the websites and their actual location, she launched the project a year after finishing school. Few knew what was going on in the basement of the foundation. Those who helped, such as lawyers around the world, had a phone number to call but could not track the location of their special project. It had to be as secret as possible to avoid sabotage and personal attacks.

All workers at the foundation were required to work one day on the farm mission with the children. It was not optional. Acelin's purpose for this rule was to keep them focused on the reason for their troubling work. Every worker was monitored carefully so that they were not caught up in the world of pornography.

Some of the work was necessarily very offensive to the soul. They had to view things that should not be viewed by anyone in order to get the information they needed. The job of the programmers and in some cases hackers was to track down the servers that made it possible to distribute the child porn on the Internet. They were primarily concerned with code. Those dealing with facial recognition were not so fortunate.

Acelin found and ordered child porn videos. They in turn watched the videos and captured facial images of the children and the abusers. These facial images were fed into the data base and the videos filed in a vault to be used as evidence if a criminal was caught.

Facial recognition software ran continuously trying to match children with missing children and criminals with most wanted posters and other records such as prison photos, passports and border crossings. Acelin gathered any new and updated software available to further enhance their efforts.

She did at the foundation what law enforcement had trouble doing. She stayed focused on one task. Stopping the industry or hampering it any way she could.

Pete suggested to a senator friend that the rules needed to be tightened on those providing servers and search engines. They should not be able to cry 'no knowledge' when criminals used their facilities to commit crimes. They should be encouraged to monitor their customers more closely so that they were not a party to a crime. It happened to some degree. Records were kept of those who actively solicited access to illegal material online. Law enforcement started to serve papers and confiscating computers from homes and businesses where there was a 'proven direct effort and systematic access' of child porn sites. From this effort, it was possible to supena credit card payments and track the money to wherever the trail led. The public grew leery of going to such websites and more leery in making payments to them. It put a big dent in the profitability of the business. The criminals, always resourceful, did figure out ways to circumvent paying directly to the porn site. They would set up a legal but useless business where the member had to pay a membership fee. Their membership identification would then give them access to the porn material and thus cloud the money trail. The embarrassment of having federal agents come into their home and explain to the family why the computer was being taken was enough to stop most people from being customers of the insidious criminals.

Border crossing photos were particularly fruitful. Instead of taking the drivers word for it, all occupants of vehicles were required to pass through a check point where security cameras captured their images. These images were cleaned up and fed into the database. License plates were cross-referenced. Although, border guards could not detain the people without cause, if the computer got a hit, an Amber alert could be issued for the child and the vehicle. Recreational vehicles received visual checks for hidden passengers. Trucks could not be searched front to back but heat sensing equipment was used which gave some degree of knowledge about its contents, unless measures were taken to conceal body heat.

Acelin was not above bending the law to stop child abuse if she had a good reason. She had planted a few viruses and worms of her own. Never did she ask or allow her employees to take on this task. Most knew nothing about it or were not sure. The better hackers in her employ had their ideas but kept them to themselves. Acelin could be stern at times.

So she went forward, trying to be the biggest 'pain in the neck' she could be for the criminals. She knew they were trying to locate her and the facilities but so far they had been unsuccessful.

In one of her sessions with Peter Justice and Taffy, Pete burst in a rare fit of laughter.

"I got the justice department complaining that you are giving them so much evidence and so many opportunities to catch bad guys that they cannot keep up." Pete said.

Acelin seldom laughed anymore. She was perhaps too deep into the mechanics of her efforts.

"They should hire more people." She said.

"They are the largest single employer now." Pete advised.

"Then they should have them work a full day." Acelin came back.

"You should get away from things for a while." Taffy told her.

"Too much to do." Acelin told her.

"No. You force your people to get away and clear their head. You need to take care of yourself." Taffy insisted.

"You're grumpy." Pete said with a smile.

Acelin did finally smile then. "You know. It is no wonder you are such a good lawyer. You are so honest and to the point."

"I am ain't I." He said.

"Okay. Okay. I'll get away. Where do you two want me to go." Acelin asked.

"How about some island?" Taffy told her.

"Which one? I've never left this town that I remember." She replied.

"Go where we went on our honeymoon. I'll get you the brochures." Taffy said.

"Do I have to find a husband to take?" Acelin asked with just a touch of sarcasm.

"We will work on that but they do take singles." Taffy said.

"I'll need someone to watch after things." Acelin said.

"Done." Taffy said.

"I have to make sure my people do not get drawn into some bad things." Acelin said.

"I can do that. You haven't forgotten where I came from, have you?" Taffy asked.

"I'll take Beau with me." Acelin said.

"That will keep the bad guys away." Taffy said.

"Now, let me see. Where do I *want* to go? Maybe I could visit one of those countries where the human trafficking is known to start." Acelin wondered aloud.

Pete and Taffy just looked at each other. It did not sound much like a vacation.

Epilogue

Daniel and Charis still run their mission, farm and school. It has expanded considerably. They have helped others set up similar rescue operations and have traveled to help them get started.

Pete and Taffy Justice went to visit her aged parents. They readily forgave Taffy for leaving and the four of them talked for hours.

Trunk is still in prison and probably will always be. In an unusual effort at redemption, Trunk signed over all his real estate holdings to Taffy. She in turn sold the properties and partnered with Acelin and Beau to form the foundation for children who had been thrown away, abandoned and in danger of abuse. The foundation devoted an entire floor of their office space to tracking down and reporting child abuse schemes. Beau traveled the country telling audiences how one stranger, a little girl named Acelin, picked him up off the street and made him part of her family. "If a little girl can have compassion and take on such responsibility even when she had nothing of her own, surely we can find it in our hearts to help a child." He told of Acelin's mother and the daring rescue in the child porn studio. He told of the mission and the two people who gave their life to scoop children out of the grip of death.

Matte Slithers went insane in prison and to this day still runs for president. He keeps saying something about a cartoon room. His wife and daughter never visited.

Of course, they called the foundation Mother's Coat. The glass fronted box that Daniel made, hangs as the centerpiece in the lobby of their building with Madra's coat inside. It is worn and sewn in many places. Acelin never enters the building without stopping to stand at the coat that gave her comfort through many dark and cold nights. To many it may not have looked good at all but to Acelin it was the most beautiful coat she had ever seen. It was Mother's Coat.

"Every day, approximately 1.3 million runaway, thrownaway, and homeless youth live on the streets of America" **ncfy.acf.hhs.gov.**

"And of some have compassion, making a difference:"
Jude 22

The question is this: Do street children irritate us
or break our hearts?

Writing this story and the necessary research has caused us to want to reach out to a child and we are in the process.

A simple search will reveal many organizations which are trying to do their part but they cannot accomplish their mission without individual help.

It would not be proper for me to recommend a particular organization. In my process of researching a number of websites for these organizations, I used my own criteria. I found one that believed like I do and one that was on the ground where the children are. I skipped over one where the director took a high salary. I also looked for one where most of the money went to the children and operating cost was low.

It cost somewhere around thirty dollars a month to help a child with food, shelter, school and a better opportunity to reach adulthood with fewer scars. That is less than a night out, a cable bill, a day of vacation, you get the idea. Need I say? Please help a child!

Milton J Southerland

The End